Student Activities in
American Education

THE LIBRARY OF EDUCATION

A Project of The Center for Applied Research in Education, Inc.

G. R. Gottschalk, Director

Categories of Coverage

I	II	III
Curriculum and Teaching	Administration, Organization, and Finance	Psychology for Educators

IV	V	VI
History, Philosophy, and Social Foundations	Professional Skills	Educational Institutions

Student Activities in American Education

ROBERT W. FREDERICK

Professor of Education
State University of New York
Albany

The Center for Applied Research in Education, Inc.

New York

Foreword

Dr. Frederick regards American education as a test slice of life, and student activities as a realistic part of this education. The various social, political, and recreational interests of adults are represented in student life in schools and colleges. It is this representation, its purpose, its history, its development and its philosophy, that is so carefully examined in the book, *Student Activities in American Education.*

From a background of experience as a teacher, administrator, and educational philosopher, Dr. Frederick has written an illuminating and informative treatise on student activities. The author is especially well qualified to write about activities as they have evolved in American education. His first degree was a Bachelor of Philosophy. At Yale and New York University, where he did his graduate work, Dr. Frederick studied sociology and philosophy as they influence the process and programs of education.

In this second half of the twentieth century, educationists, concerned lay citizens, and parents have been prompted to take a new look at the programs of their educational institutions. It is especially important that student activities be made a part of this reappraisal. Their growth, the problems of financing, and the allocation of costly school facilities have made the lay public as well as the professional educators concerned with the fundamental purposes and future development of student life outside the classroom.

Dr. Frederick has made a valuable reappraisal. He sees extracurricular activities as an important and valuable part of institutionalized education but is frank in pointing out errors, abuses, excesses, and important gaps. He has important suggestions for athletics, social activities, music, the dance, speech, dramatic force, debate and fraternities. Each activity has been carefully placed in the broad context of American life and in proper historical perspective.

v

Anyone concerned with the total educational picture, will do well to take advantage of this exposition which has been so carefully planned and executed.

RANDOLF GARDNER

Dean, School of Education
State University of New
York at Albany

Student Activities in
American Education

Robert W. Frederick

One of the distinctive characteristics of American education is the emphasis on nonclassroom activities. Dr. Frederick has ably presented the full range of these activities in this volume. The educational objectives of these activities are presented as the theme around which the book is constructed. Each chapter includes both a presentation of the student activity and a careful analysis.

The reader gets the full sweep of this aspect of the school program as he views student self-government, the communication arts, the performing arts, social activities, athletics, and sororities and fraternities. Dr. Frederick has termed this multitude of experiences *the third curriculum*. This term might well be preferred to earlier titles such as *extracurriculum* or *cocurriculum*, since these activities are so well integrated into the daily school program.

No reader will leave this book feeling that student activities are frills; rather, he will have a high estimation of their educational value. Those who feel that the development of skill in working in groups, the cultivation of hobbies and interests, and the production of plays, yearbooks, newspapers are satisfying experiences will agree with Dr. Frederick that *the third curriculum* has its proper place in American education.

Dr. Robert W. Frederick is Professor of Education at the College of Education of the State University of New York. He has been principal of the Milne School, a campus school at the College of Education. He has viewed student activities as a parent, as a principal, and as a professor. There are few people as well qualified as he to write this Library of Education volume.

DANIEL E. GRIFFITHS
Content Editor

Contents

CONTENTS

CHAPTER VIII

A Look Ahead   92

Bibliography   105

Index   109

Student Activities in
American Education

CHAPTER I

School Society and American Society

Every society and all the subcultures within each make some provision for leading the young from the careless freedom of childhood to the full and responsible participation as an adult in the affairs of the group. In simple cultures the process is brief, sometimes cruel, but usually straightforward. In primitive cultures, the child is taught to ride, to shoot, to stalk game, and to respect the traditions of his tribe; and all this is done by his father or, perhaps, by an elder brother. In complex societies, the process is longer, more complicated, and more highly organized and systematized. To these more complex procedures is given the generic term *education*. In advanced societies education is deliberate, planned, and institutionalized; it is carried on, far from the family hearth, by specialists called *teachers* and *professors*, and managed by hierarchies of administrators, boards of control, ministers, and legislators.

The complexity of the culture makes it necessary to devote much attention to the content taught and to introduce procedures which are of less and less immediate use in the real world. Meaningful use of much of the formalized curriculum is therefore necessarily delayed, and the value of a great part of what youth has to learn in the classroom is vague, remote, problematic, and contingent.

The student's nonclassroom activities, on the other hand, are of real and immediate importance. College student riots and spring panty raids are, in part, a reaction against the delayed values of the academic curriculums. Professor Rudolph[1] maintains that college student activities were introduced by students to make physical exercise and the intellectual discussion of issues a part of college life. Whatever the reason, it is a fact that in such activities students

---

[1] Frederick Rudolph, *The American College and University* (New York: Alfred A. Knopf, Inc., 1962). Chap. 5, "The Collegiate Way" and Chap. 7, "The Extracurriculum" are especially valuable. See also Chap. 18, "The Rise of Football."

find meaning *now*. The Festival of the Arts *has* to be ready next weekend—and it will be enjoyed next Saturday night, not five or six years from now. Art exhibits, publication deadlines, new around-end-option plays for the next game—these are as immediate to modern youth as the stalking of game for the evening meal was to the Indian youth of early America.

The evolution and development of American educational policy and processes in the early decades of the twentieth century were not simply a reaction to or against the European pattern. Indigenous American educational patterns have their roots in prior innovations, in earlier turning points that were in their time significant and controversial. The shift from Latin to the language of the community, from the concept of education as an arm of the church to that of education as an instrument of the state, from private to public support, from the authority of the ancients to the rule of evidence, from the criterion of mental "discipline" to that of the useful, from a preoccupation with the past to a concern for the future— not all of these may be labeled *Made in the USA*.

During the first three decades of this century, however, Americans in town meetings and school meetings did create a new concept of education. This native American concept of schooling was most dramatically manifested in the secondary schools. It was pragmatic, instrumental, pluralistic, relativistic, and experimental. It made the school the equal of the home and the church as a social agency. This new concept of education has been spelled out in innumerable documents. John Dewey is usually given the credit (or blame) for this concept, but he did not invent it; he only put into words the philosophy and beliefs of the American people.

New American educational concepts replaced and reinterpreted such hallowed traditions as the "discipline" of mental faculties, the "automatic" transfer of training, knowledge for knowledge's sake, "single" standards of excellence, prestige hierarchies of subjects, curriculum absolutes, the mind as a "vessel," and the monopoly of the verbalism of the idealists. New ideas were used to guide the new education. These new American-made concepts were in keeping with the spirit of the American tradition, not the European. Direct value, learning by doing, specificity, universality, the whole person—these became the guiding principles of the new education.

In all this philosophic adventuring, student activities played a very significant part. When school life was made an extension of home and community life and the many new facets were added to academic and vocational institutions, new concepts of curriculum, educational aims and methods, and the teaching role were necessary. In 1918,[2] the educational aims restated by the Kingsley committee of the National Education Association included health, good citizenship, effective use of leisure, ethical and moral character, home membership, and vocational competency as well as the fundamental skills. Curriculum was redefined to include all activities that influence the way others think, feel, believe, and act. Dances, teas, ballgames, chess, and all the many recreational activities became media of introduction in the values and virtues of democratic life. What the aristocrats—the Adams, the Washingtons, the Jeffersons—enjoyed should be the privilege of all.

In keeping with the new views of the role of schools and colleges, a new educational structure was evolved. Under the leadership of Charles W. Eliot of Harvard, credit curriculums were split into required, or constant courses, and widely varied elective offerings from which the student might choose. The required curriculum was modified to retain only those subjects considered of value to all the children from all American homes. The elective curriculum retained the traditional mathematical, linguistic and science subjects. To these were added new subjects and new sequences. The aim was to meet the interests and needs of as many young people as possible. At the college level the elective curriculums became "schools of," "departments of," or "divisions of" everything and anything important to the American people, including hotel management and labor relations.

Student activities, now a part of the American educative process, constitute what will be called *the third curriculum*. Student activities lie in the noncredit part of institutional education. In general, an activity may be classified as a student activity if it is voluntarily engaged in, if it is approved and supervised by a member of the professional staff, and if it carries no credit toward promotion, certification, or graduation. The dividing line between the credit and the noncredit curriculums is not sharp, for some activities—for example, assemblies—are mandatory in many schools.

---

[2] Commission on the Reorganization of Secondary Education, *Cardinal Principles of Education*, Bulletin No. 35 (Washington, D.C.: USGPO, 1918).

Professor Cox[3] said in 1924 that a better name than *extracurricular activities* was needed. Many different terms have since been used. There is some reason to believe that *student activities* and *cocurriculum* will be the ones generally employed. But the term suggested here, *the third curriculum,* may be used by professional educationists, for it puts this important part of American education in its proper context.

[3] See Phillip W. Cox, *Creative School Control* (Philadelphia: J. B. Lippincott Company, 1926), for an early analysis of the extracurriculum.

CHAPTER II

Student Self-Government

In the twentieth century, the dominant position in the affairs of men is held by the nation-state. Governments, politicians, and politics thus become the arbiters of human affairs. At one extreme, as in the totalitarian states, government is controlled by one man or by a small group of men. In the Western democracies it is the many who have the decisive voice and who wield the all-inclusive power of the state for or against the general welfare.

The battle for the control of the lives and fortunes of the many men in the many streets of the world never ends. Kings and peers of the realm, government leaders, the clergy, the military, and the industrial complex struggle for dominance. In all cases today, it is those who run the government who win. The state, however constituted, is the agency which taxes, spends, plans, and rules. As Knight[1] says, modern intellectuals who are not interested in politics are like the thirteenth-century professors who were not interested in science.

Citizenship and patriotism become then the dominant, all-embracing aims of education for *the state*. Education is defined by whoever has the power to requisition funds, services, and materials. Deliberate education—public, private, or parochial—has become an arm of the state and a weapon against rival states.

America is the custodian, if not the originator, of the thesis that governments are the creatures and the servants of the people. Lincoln's *of the people, by the people, and for the people* is more than an apt turn of phrase: it is a way of life for Americans. A French king could declare, "I am the state." Americans have been taught to believe "We are the state."

That this idea is of transcendent importance no American would deny. The hackneyed phrases: *liberty, freedom, equality, justice,* and *right* have real meaning. These treasured concepts naturally and properly are extended into the relationship of adults and young people in schools and colleges.

---

[1] Everett Knight, *The Objective Society* (New York: George Braziller, Inc., 1960).

5

American youth are early inducted into the never quite perfected realms of freedom, personal responsibility, individual dignity, self-determination, and right of individual choice. It did not require a French philosopher to expound that existence precedes essence for American parents to conclude that self-choice and self-direction begin in early childhood. The Hebraic doctrine of the supremacy of the father (with the power of life and death over his children) does not work in a society in which the test of excellence is success—not rank, title, or station. The ability to ride, to shoot, to chop wood, to trade horses, *to do,* and *to produce* led quite naturally to the practice of measuring the individual, not according to his station, but according to his abilities.

To test worth through ability, individuality, and responsibility rather than through age, title, wealth, position, or piety, translated into practice, means that American youth—at home and at school—are permitted and encouraged to take over the management of their own affairs as rapidly as possible (and sometimes faster than is desirable).

Student government, or student participation in self-government, is a logical and natural feature of American education. If men are to be free, the young too must learn what it means to be free.

Long before parents were convinced that the young should be given a weekly allowance to manage for themselves and that they should be taught to live with their own mistakes in judgment, American schools were experimenting with rudimentary forms of student government. Yet it is a fact that even today some schools and colleges exercise an Old World type of supervision. In many institutions of higher learning, young adults are hedged about with rules and regulations. They are told, or ordered, not to miss classes on penalty of double cuts; they are faced with locked doors and faculty wrath if they return from dances or dates after the established hour. It is a curious fact that, as late as 1960, the large men's private colleges in the East put more trust in student judgment than did the teachers colleges.

History

As early as the sixteenth century the College of William and Mary (1779) and the William Penn Charter School (1777) were experimenting with rudimentary forms of student government, as were Eton and Rugby (1786) in England. In 1819, the University of Virginia established a form of student control. Early ventures were also made at Wattakeseett School of Duxbury, Massachusetts (1840), the Evanston College for Ladies (1873), and at Hartford public schools (1852). The very liberal George Junior Republic was established in 1894 at Freeville, New York, under the leadership of William George.[2]

All the attempts were made in the conviction that the young must be given experience in freedom if they are to be free as adults; all were sporadic and short-lived. It was not until the twentieth century that Americans finally decided to break with the European tradition of education that student government became a widespread way of school and college life. The progressive doctrines of learning by doing, education as preparation for life, direct practice, and the denial of general mental discipline did not succeed in changing the methods of the classroom and the content of the curriculum except in its grosser phases. They did, however, have full play in the newer American system of student activities, and especially in student responsibility for self-government.

With the tremendous increase in high school enrollments and in the number of high schools after the turn of the century, the number of student associations for participation in self-government increased rapidly. There was no Old Guard scholastic tradition to impede the growth of student government as there was in the credit courses of history, languages, mathematics, and the others. By 1926, E. V. Rugg[3] could report that 90 per cent of American high schools had some form of student government. As early as 1931, the National Association of Student Offices was founded; in 1943 it was placed under the sponsorship of the National Association of Secondary School Principals and renamed the National Association of Student Councils.

It is safe to say that by the middle of the century practically all the schools and colleges in America recognized the practical and

---

[2] See Harry C. McKown, *The Student Council* (New York: McGraw-Hill Book Company, 1944).

[3] See Paul W. Terry, *Supervising Extracurricular Activities* (New York: McGraw-Hill Book Company, 1930) and *The Encyclopedia of Educational Research*, 3rd ed., ed., Chester W. Harris (N.Y.: The Macmillan Company, 1960), for an extended discussion of historical development.

theoretical values of systematic participation on the part of students in the management of their affairs. The principle has won almost universal acceptance. Many men in high public office were once prominent figures in the student governments of their schools and colleges. This is not to imply that mistakes were not made, nor that in many schools *student government* was not merely an empty phrase. But the doctrine that the ways of freedom must be learned by practice in real situations became firmly established in the schools of the nation.

Aims and Functions

American educators have made almost a fetish of objectives in spite of the fact that men and their wives eat, sleep, love, have children, and worship without ever—or only very rarely—asking "Why?"

The reasons for the existence of student councils or some form of student organization for self-control go deep into American history. This is not the time or place to trace that bit of Americana. Schools and colleges have student councils because they are useful in doing jobs that need to be done—because they fill an obvious need.

To the much-maligned educationists, student participation in self-government is essential in the preservation of the high ideals of Western democracy. In conventional terms, student councils are a part of education for citizenship; basic to all student organizations is the doctrine that the young are citizens, that citizenship is conferred at birth, not at age eighteen or twenty-one. Whether participation in student government contributes more to citizenship education than learning the facts of American history is not our concern. It is sufficient to say that practice in citizenship is one way to assure that the student will be a good citizen as an adult.

To the students the aim of student government is to do some jobs that need to be done. If it is the students' wish to invite a foreign student, the student government provides a vehicle for proposing the idea, for discussing it, for making the final decision and for appropriating the money. It becomes a project of, by, and for students. In the American tradition, those affected by the decision should make the decision. Students have enterprises which are important to them and, all too often perhaps, of excessive importance to their parents. That they should manage, support, and evaluate their enterprises is so natural and logical to American youth that they give no thought to justifying this freedom.

Student organizations for self-government of student affairs are charged with initiating, supervising, regulating, financing, and evaluating student enterprises which do not carry official credits for graduation, college entrance, or judgments of vocational competence. The student aim is a practical affair: to get things done. It is in the American tradition of the active virtues: build, make, do.

The objectives of student government, in educational terms, include all the approved value aims of education. The list can be expanded endlessly: responsibility, initiative, leadership, fellowship, self-control, self-reliance, cooperation, respect for law and order, honesty, obedience to law, and effective citizenship. It is sufficient to say that student councils are useful—if guided by competent persons—in developing the basis for and the ideals of good citizenship.

Activities

The activities of the student councils in the promotion of the general school and national welfare are as varied as are the interests of Americans—particularly American youth. The students in any given community reflect the level of thinking of the people of the community. If the students of the Bethlehem Central School decide to adopt a foreign student, it is clear that the people of the community have manifested—and transmitted to their children—some sense of global responsibility. The specific activities of the student council depend very definitely and revealingly on the level of citizenship in the community. The role of the school authorities is to encourage the student council to undertake those activities which will lead to the better types of social thought and action.

Student councils have a decisive role and an advisory role. The decisive role requires that procedures for resolving problems between students and administration be outlined in the constitution. The advisory role is exercised at the request of the school authorities or when an issue arises in which the students feel they have a vital interest. The higher the social awareness of the students and the more developed their social skills, the more frequently will their judgment be sought.

The decision-making responsibilities of the student council are restricted to the noncredit curriculums, or the student activities. The council is the chief managing body in this phase of institutional life. Directly or indirectly, all clubs, publications, social affairs, sports (outside the required physical education) and dramatic activities should exist at the will of the council and should be regulated and evaluated by the council.[4] In terms of range of concern and amount of responsibility, the council—representing the whole student body and the public—is itself the major student activity. It will not receive as much notice as does the basketball team, and it will not, except at the installation ceremony, receive public applause; but its work will affect all students and many homes in the community.

The common treatment of student council activities is to make long lists of specific things some school councils do or have done. These lists are as long as the patience of the investigator—for one or another of the student councils has done everything from commissioning the writing of a school song—with a money prize for the winning composer—to polishing the school trophies and cleaning the glass display case.

Miller, Moyer, and Patrick[5] after a survey of the number of schools, listed many "examples . . . of activities promoted by councils that have been recommended as exemplifying 'best practices,' for the purpose of suggesting ideas which may be helpful to other councils."

In operational terms student councils perform the services common to administrative bodies. The president of the council acts as an administrator, president, superintendent, chief executive, or board chairman. They do what, in their best judgment, needs to be done to insure the success of the total enterprise and each separate contributing activity.

1. They conduct studies, investigations, and research projects. They carry on problem-solving activities. They gather data, facts, and opinions on selected issues or proposals and use these as the basis for reaching de-

---

[4] Compare with the rise of the nation-state or government alluded to on p. 5.
[5] F. A. Miller, J. H. Moyer, and R. B. Patrick, *Planning Student Activities* (Englewood Cliffs, N.J.: Prentice-Hall, Inc., 1956), pp. 257–61.

cisions. The factors common to human issues—cost, public opinion, gain, time and energy demands, relative value—enter into the effort in proportion to the magnitude of the question or problem.

2. They make decisions and settle issues.
3. They delegate responsibility.
4. They initiate, promote, innovate, lead.
5. They consult.
6. They supervise, and give or secure help.
7. They coordinate, integrate, and articulate the diverse and inevitably complicated programs.
8. They look ahead and anticipate needs and difficulties.
9. They inform.
10. They evaluate.

A word must be said here about the police powers or disciplinary responsibilities of the student association's administrative body. Upper-classmen in a military academy may quite properly be given large powers to whip first-year students into officers and gentlemen, for military academies are special-purpose institutions. It is clear that a general-purpose school or college should leave the handling of transgressions against school and community law (theft, truancy, cheating, drunkenness) to school and police authorities. Neglect or inefficiency in performing properly delegated student services can and should be handled by the students.

Qualifications of Council Members

If these administrative and supervisory activities are to be effectively performed, a set of contributory skills and traits will have to be developed. Council members among other things must be able to:

1. Speak clearly and concisely to small and large groups;
2. Write clearly and concisely;
3. Work in groups;
4. Chair meetings;
5. Influence, persuade, and convince;
6. Use status authority;
7. Exercise moral and intellectual authority;
8. Distribute praise and blame justly;
9. Think straight.

In addition to such desirable human traits as tact, honesty, emotional balance, and a sense of humor, student council members should be:

1. Problem-centered;
2. Objective;
3. Nonappetitive;
4. Perceptive, insightful, inventive;
5. Personnel-minded, respectful of others;
6. Autonomous, self-confident;
7. Relativistic, pluralistic.

It should be obvious that perfection is so rare as to be, for practical purposes, nonexistent. The gap between *is* and *ought*—between the desirable and the attainable—is wide and deep. Students, like other people, have compensatory strengths which to some extent make up for their inevitable and obvious shortages.

Organizations—Structures

Students' participation in the management of their lives in educational institutions designed to guide their passage from childhood to adulthood has undergone great changes since the days of ancient Athens and Sparta. As the concept of secondary education changed in the twentieth century, so have there been corresponding changes in the structure and organization of student affairs.

Student organizations are elaborate and simple, legalistic and natural, imitative and original. They are all generally representative; they all work under a constitution and include a complement of officers. Many older organizations are as burdened by tradition as is the Congress of the United States. But organization and structure are means, not ends. They are important, however, for in the American ideology the *how* is part of the *what* and the *why*.

Representatives to the student council are selected in a variety of ways. The general representation of a relatively permanent group (such as a homeroom, a class, or a grade group) is preferred over the special representation of officers of suborganizations.

Appointment of representatives to the legislative and administrative body is not widely practiced. Representatives are commonly elected by free, secret ballot, more and more frequently by the use of public voting machines. Eligibility for membership is nonrestrictive; it is based on membership in the student body. Some general organizations do specify that representatives must be in a certain grade group, have a definite level of scholarship, adhere to standards of good citizenship, and be relatively free of other responsibilities. In general, the wider concept of eligibility is preferred for the very important reason that it is desirable for all students to have the opportunity to practice the exercise of judgment.

Nomination of representatives to the general organization or of candidates for student council offices is ordinarily left to the group represented. The party system has not developed except in a few larger universities.

In many schools the election campaigns are conducted in the manner of political campaigns for public office. Restrictions as to the spending of money, the display of posters, and the length of the campaign are common. Campaign managers are selected by candidates, and campaign speeches are delivered at an election assembly.

The complement of officers includes a president, vice-president, secretary, treasurer, and sometimes a parliamentarian. These officers may be elected by the delegates to the council or by the student body as a whole. In the latter case they may or may not be members of the council. If they are not, they generally automatically become so upon election.

The unicameral legislative council is common. In 1954, the students at Fordham University adopted a bicameral structure for their student government; it was reported to be the only one in the country. Frederick Reuss, a senior at the university and chairman of the constitutional committee, reported in *The New York Times:* "We have worked for six months to see this thing in operation. I think we read the constitution of every major school in the country before we decided to be completely different."[6]

School governments have taken as their models the mayoral and manager types of city government, state governments, and the federal government. The trend is generally toward locally devised structures. In the early twentieth century, very elaborate legalistic, imitative organizations with elaborate constitutions were established. In later decades, the trend has been toward a more simple, natural structure. The emphasis has been placed on a simple beginning and a gradual growth in complexity of organization as successive

---

[6] *The New York Times,* March 14, 1954.

generations of students mature and their duties and responsibilities broaden.

OATH OF STUDENT COUNCIL

I, _____, having been elected a member of the Xville Junior Council, do solemnly state that I shall uphold and obey all rules and regulations of the Xville School. I further pledge that I shall do all in my power to make Xville College stand high.

The elections, usually held in the spring, are followed by an induction ceremony. These may be elaborate or casual. In either case they are important, for the new council will reflect the tone of the ceremony. Parents are sometimes invited and the press is given the story.

Special identification items—pins, armbands, or some other visible symbol—are sometimes presented. An "oath" may be administered. The president of the council may give a keynote speech which is similar in tone to the inaugural address of an incoming President of the United States.

The total student activities program may be divided into several categories,[7] each of which may then be put under the direction of a board of policy and control. In such a system, the general council divides the responsibility for the day-to-day administration and supervision of the various activities among a number of separate subgroups. Each subgroup outlines the policy, manages, supervises, and evaluates a set of related student enterprises. This subdivision of responsibility increases efficiency by reducing the number of persons who report directly to the president and the general council. The number of such subgroups is directly related to the size of the school and the scope of the student activity program.

The management of human affairs is, at any level, a grave responsibility. It is also a complex duty. In many states specific programs have been initiated to "educate" boards of education in their duties and responsibilities. In this same spirit, a few schools have instituted systematic procedures for the education of student council officers and members. In Bakersfield, California, this service is part of the social studies curriculum. By such programs, edu-

---

[7] See Robert W. Frederick, *The Third Curriculum* (New York: Appleton-Century-Crofts, Inc., 1959), Chap. II and Appendix B for a discussion of the need for classification of student activities and a suggested detailed classification.

cation in free, democratic, and responsible leadership is regularized.

Student government is a way to get many necessary things done. Its supporting role in citizenship education is as yet only partially appreciated. The extent to which instruction by the faculty will be helpful and the degree to which it interferes with learning by doing and by making mistakes depends on the wisdom and skill of the faculty. Of course, everything does depend on the quality of instruction. In the case of student government, however, this point is critical.

The student council and the officers of the general organization need time and a place to carry on their work. Offices, desks, meeting rooms, file cabinets, typewriters, and secretarial services are important to effective work and to the development of authority and respect. Student organization personnel carry out their duties in their spare time. Their duties are important and often time-consuming. For these reasons, ability and time are important desiderta which the electorate must consider. As various studies have shown, student council officers and members are almost invariably elected from the more intelligent, academically successful, and socially acceptable school citizens.

Procedures

The responsibilities of the faculty in the noncredit student activities are many and varied—but they are all important, for the educative value of student activities is important. High on the list should be the maintenance of orderly procedures in group discussion and decision-making. The role of the chairman is critical, but all members of the group have the responsibility to follow accepted rules of parliamentary order and courtesy. Parliamentary procedures are well established, and any number of rule books are available for student use. Some are specifically prepared for high school students.

The order in which business is to be considered is generally outlined in the constitution or by-laws of the organization. It can be straightforward and without elaborate details:

1. Call to order;
2. Roll call;
3. Determination of a quorum;
4. Reports of officers and active committees;

5. Old, unfinished business;
6. New business;
7. Adjournment.

Under Items 4, 5, and 6, the presiding officer should have prepared a list of the items to be discussed, in the order of their importance. This list should be made available to all council members some days before the meeting.

Parliamentary procedures can be relatively simple. There is ordinarily no need to employ the complexities of questions of privilege, points of order, the limitation or extension of debate, and the like. Beyond the usual rules of order, a sense of purpose, a respect for order, and—above all—common courtesy are of paramount importance. Wisecracking, attempts at humor, and impulsive exclamations of approval or disagreement should be discouraged. Certainly the attention of the group should be centered on the person who is talking and distractions should not be tolerated. Class meetings are all too often prone to disorder and confusion. A tradition of order and courtesy can be developed.

Years ago Vineyard and Poole[8] listed what they termed the "Commandments of Parliamentary Usage." They deserve the consideration of all student council members.

Affiliations

America has no national system of education. It has fifty separate and autonomous state systems. But there is a great deal of *de facto,* if not *de jure,* commonality in school practices from Maine to Hawaii. This comes about through the efforts of a variety of agencies, including the National Education Association and its many affiliated organizations.

Student government, as one phase of American education, is no exception. Local, regional, state, and national organizations have been established on the secondary school[9] and college levels.

---

[8] J. J. Vineyard and C. F. Poole, *Student Participation in School Government* (New York: A. S. Barnes and Co., 1930), p. 104.

[9] For the best and most complete coverage of student councils or student government in the high schools of the United States, see *The Student Council in the Secondary School: A Handbook for Student Councils and Their Advisers* (Washington, D.C.: The National Association of Secondary School Principals, 1962).

These organizations are directed to mutual assistance in improving student life and education in general.

Among the several organizations are the many regional student government groups. The schools of an area, as a county or city, are increasingly forming associations for the exchange of ideas. They hold one or two meetings per year. The sponsors meet together to consider common problems. The students hold their own meetings to exchange ideas. The host school makes the necessary arrangements, but the agenda is set by the district officers.

The state associations of student councils are growing in number. The work of these associations is illustrated by a news item which stated:

> Miss Emily Barker, . . . has been elected president of the State Association of Student Councils. She is a junior at Scotia-Glenville High School where she is active in student organization . . . Miss Barker will attend the conference on juvenile delinquency at the State Education building tomorrow. She will also be a junior staff member at a leadership training institute June 24–28 sponsored by Syracuse University and the state student group.

Gerald Van Pool, Director of Student Activities, National Education Association, described the development of the National Association of Student Councils:[10]

> In 1931, at the National Education Association in Los Angeles, Dr. Willis A. Sutton, NEA president, suggested that there might be a national association of those interested in student council work. Acting upon his suggestion, a number of students and teachers did meet and made plans for such an association. Rather small groups met with the NEA at its regular conventions until the start of World War II when the national meetings were discontinued. In 1943, negotiations were started between the teachers in charge of what was then called the *National Association of Student Officers* and the National Association of Secondary School Principals. The result of these negotiations was that the National Association of Secondary School Principals agreed to assume direction of student councils on a national scale as one of its *major* projects. At that time, there were *283* schools on the mailing list of the old association. The name was changed to the *National Association of Student Councils* and since then membership has grown until now there are

---

[10] Gerald Van Pool, "Vitalizing Student Activities," *Bulletin of the National Association of Secondary-School Principals,* Vol. 36, No. 184 (February 1952). Reprinted by permission from the *Bulletin of the National Association of Secondary School Principals,* February 1952. Copyright: Washington, D.C.

over 5200 schools enrolled. The association has published eleven books on the student council. In 1947, the membership had grown so large that it was necessary to add another staff member and the position of *Director of Student Activities* was created. Any school needing information on any phase of student council work should write to the

National Association of Student Councils
1201 Sixteenth Street, N.W.
Washington 6, D.C.

The College National Student Association held its first meeting in Chicago in 1946, representing a large segment of American college students. A. Blair Knapp, President of Denison University, asked in 1953: "Isn't it time we accept it as an opportunity to strengthen the concept that students are citizens of the college community and, as such, have much to contribute to the community government of the college?" In 1957 *The New York Times* editorialized:

> A nonpartisan, nonsectarian confederation, the U.S.N.S.A. represents more than *800,000* American students through their democratically elected campus governments at 350 colleges and universities. In its first ten years of existence, the association has given expression to student opinion, has sought to increase the students' responsibility and contribution to the college community and has worked to strengthen relations between American students and students in other countries. The association has also bitterly opposed efforts to limit academic freedom both in this country and in other nations.

Today the National Student Association represents over a million college students from more than 400 colleges in all parts of the country. It has sponsored programs designed to increase faculty salaries, to recruit college teachers, and to increase faculty salaries, to recruit college teachers, and to increase the effectiveness of teaching and curriculums. It sponsors visits by foreign student leaders and assists individuals and groups in foreign study and travel.

The Advisor or Faculty Representative

If, as commonly accepted, citizenship in a free democracy is the overarching aim of public education and if, as is generally agreed, student self-government is the keystone of the total student activity program, then the role of the faculty's representative is of maximum significance. No other position carries more opportunity or more responsibility. The faculty advisor generally works with school leaders who exercise status and moral leadership in the conduct of the public business. What is done and how it is done sets patterns of action and ideals of responsible citizenship which will become the patterns and ideals of the next generation of citizens.

The advisor to the student council should be appointed by the chief administator of the school or by his assistant. Theoretically, students should elect their chief advisor, just as the people elect their chief executive. The fact is, of course, that few student bodies are mature enough to make this decision. In time, popular election may be possible as well as desirable, but in most cases that time has not arrived.

The duties of the faculty advisor are highly specialized. The student council is a deliberative and decision-making body—in some instances it refers decisions, with or without recommendation, to the total school citizenry. The advisor is, in a very real sense, a director of group thinking. He teaches the group how to think in real situations. All the complexities of emotional commitment, community reaction, administrative bias, and personality differences are present. The inevitable need to clarify all issues, to gather all the facts possible, and to miss no facet of the problem is always present. The advisor properly does not point out what is right, wrong, desirable, or undersirable action, but what is the best process for arriving at a decision. The thinking and deciding are done by the students—always, of course, within their constitutional powers.

Part of the re-examination of the philosophy and process of American education which began after the launching of Sputnik I was, in effect, a re-evaluation of the desirability and the ways of introducing specialization into teaching. By the early decades of the twentieth century, teachers (except at the graduate school level) had become generalists: they were lecturers, testers, discussion leaders, social counselors, and a host of other things. Team teaching was suggested as one way to utilize the specialized competencies of individual teachers.

This idea of specialization was, of course, not new, for the blanket license to teach any high school or college subject had long since disappeared as public policy. The first specialization in student activities was in athletics. Music and dramatics soon followed. It may now be time to think of the advisor to the student council as a highly specialized role requiring special aptitudes, traits, skills, and knowledge.

McKown[11] and others have listed qualities which should be possessed by the student council faculty advisor. These include such desirable attributes as sympathy with the ideas of student government, loyalty to students and the administration, ability to win confidence and respect, a sense of humor, a sense of relative values, courage to allow some mistakes to be made by students, a genuine spirit of cooperation, resistance to discouragement, a genius for listening, courage to try the new and different, and a desire to learn.

It goes without saying that the faculty advisor should be intelligent, interested, devoted, and dedicated. Ideally, the sponsor should be, in Maslow's terms, "a healthy, self-actualizing personality." Beyond these qualities, which are desirable in all human beings, the advisor to the student government should possess very special skills and knowledges.

The specialized knowledges and skills required by the advisor to the student council are related to group processes and problem-solving procedures. Problem-solving, or thinking, is a part of every teacher's training and background. In science, psychology, methods, and philosophy, consideration is given to how one thinks. Many teacher-education programs include a required course in research methods. But only in the 1950's did studies in the field of group dynamics become the concern of educationists. Few teachers in service as late as the middle 1960's had any contact with this rapidly growing field of inquiry.

Of the need for attention to this new field Bienenstok[12] wrote:

To prevent a decline of democratic functions people must learn how to work effectively together in groups in spite of differences of opinion, expectation, and experience. Ways of reaching an agreement through mutual understanding and sharing in the diagnosis and solution of

---

[11] H. C. McKown, *The Student Council* (New York: McGraw-Hill Book Company, 1944). See also Miller, *et al., op. cit.*

[12] Theodore Bienenstok, "Impact of Social and Economic Forces on Education, III," *Group Dynamics and the Classroom Situation* (Albany, N.Y.: State Education Department, 1952).

critical problems simply have to be improved . . . Since the school accepts the preparation of young people for competent membership in a democratic society as one of its basic responsibilities, educators have the obligation to examine closely the findings of group dynamics.

This is not the time and place for a review of the findings of research in the young science of group dynamics. The advisor to the student council, it was suggested earlier, should be a specialist. One of his first duties should be to dig into this growing field of knowledge. All that can be done here is to suggest recourse to the literature in the field. Studies include very elaborate team research into a wide range of problems—from the authoritarian, fascistic personality to problem-solving in small groups of structural open and close-minded individuals.

Guiding Principles

Out of the experience of thousands of students, teachers, and administrators with responsible student government there has emerged a set of organizational and operational guidelines, on which there is wide agreement. This agreement has come about through no authoritarian edict, but in the professional exchange of ideas and experiences.

1. Student organizations, through which students may participate in managing their informal school life, fill very real and necessary functions. They are needed to teach citizenship on the action level, to give practice in developing skills in group action, and to care for the many details which must be handled if social, athletic, and other activities are to be carried on without adding to the budget for professional services. These needs are not sporadic or artificial; they are continuous and real.

2. Students and faculties must appreciate the value of the services performed by the student organization. No spirit of play-acting should permeate any phase of the work. Elections of representatives, for example, need not be grim, but they must be taken seriously. Whether a solemn, swearing-in ceremony of officers and representatives is used is incidental to the central idea—such events may be helpful in fostering a spirit of responsibility, but the total attitude in all related activities at all times is the only certain way to insure the necessary diligence. It is, of course, vitally important

that student decisions be honored by the faculty and administration of the school.

3. Representation must be total, truly representative, and known by all. Each member of the central administrative body, whatever its form or title, should represent a known group and be known by the group, report to the group, and at all times be instructed by the group. This principle means that the "local district" should be a continuing and operating group. Its members must be together regularly and for an appreciable length of time, and must continue as a group for the duration of the term of office of its elected representatives. Generally, the homeroom group, because of its size and nature, is used as the electing body, but the social studies classes can also be used.

4. A corollary to Principle 3 is that every student is a voting citizen of the school. There should be no exclusions for low marks, nonapproved behavior, or any other cause. All enrolled students are citizens of the school, and there is no loss of citizenship possible where there are no prisons and no dishonorable discharges. Enrollment in school means, if nothing else, that the student is performing in all ways at least at a minimum acceptable level.

5. Every enrolled student is eligible for election to the representative body and the administrative staff. Race, color, national origin, intelligence, social class, athletic ability, and scholarship are all irrelevant factors in determining eligibility. The fitness of any particular student for the role is another question and one which the students themselves must decide. The decision is so important that provision should be made for a discussion of the issues.

6. Student councils should be given power of decision in defined areas. These should be clearly stated in the constitution. What concerns lie within the decision-making powers of the student organization is a critical decision. Responsibility without power is a myth. It is important that the area of power grow with the students' growth in maturity and experience. It goes without saying that within the foreseeable future many decisions will lie outside the province of students, but all school and colleges are far from the possible limits at this time.

7. Student councils should be given advisory roles in selected affairs as, for example, a shift from the two- to three-semester

school year. In general, these will be handled by ad hoc committees or other deliberative agencies.

8. The role of the administrator or faculty advisor is not that of a veto-wielder, but that of a guide and helper. In a sense, he is a problem-solving aide, not the ultimate decision-maker. At rare times, the faculty may be called upon to interpret the constitution to decide whether a contemplated action falls rightly within the province of the students, whether it is in the realm of advisement, or whether it lies completely outside the realm of student considera-tion. In ordinary cases, however, the so-called veto power should disappear.

9. The student organization should be the most important and most general of all student groups. That is to say, all other activi-ties and organizations should exist and be maintained at the will of the student council and under its general supervision.

10. The structure of the student council is important but sec-ondary to the principles suggested above.

CHAPTER III

Communication Arts

Publications

Communication is the lifeblood of man as a social animal. Communication—whether through shrugs or through satellites—is the basis of civilization. Much of man's history is written in his struggles to improve communication. From the Greek runner at Marathon to Telestar, man has constantly sought to improve his contacts with his fellow men.

Under the American educational rationale, what is important in life becomes a part of schooling—for to be a student is to be alive, a citizen-in-training for responsible adulthood. The freedom of the press and of assembly are democratic recognition of the right to know, to be informed, to persuade, and to be persuaded.

Communication—or the exertion of influence on the way others think, feel, and act—takes many forms. Flags, trumpets, banners can communicate moods. The communication arts, as the phrase is used in education and generally are the means of *mass communication*. The printed word in its many forms and the spoken word are the instrumentation of mass communication. That this is a narrow use of the term is not of concern here, except that some specialized ways of communication have been neglected that should be more thoughtfully exploited in schools and colleges.

The list below suggests the range of activities in the communication arts in America's schools and colleges. Not all institutions have all forms, but, in general, schools and colleges have

1. A yearbook or annual;
2. A literary magazine;
3. A humor magazine;
4. A student handbook;
5. Newspapers;
6. Special publications:
   (a) Homeroom papers;
   (b) Class papers;

    (c) Departmental reports;
    (d) Posters;
    (e) Signs;
    (f) Bulletin boards;
    (g) News releases in the public press;
    (h) Student-written columns in the press;
    (i) Twenty-five-year classbooks;
    (j) Movies (of important events of the year);
    (k) Radio stations;
    (l) A freshman's guide to courses.

The benefits of acquaintance with and actual experience in getting out a newspaper or maintaining a bulletin board are important, for communication is important. All activities give the student an opportunity to learn responsibility, accuracy, and other esteemed virtues, but experience with publications give a unique not otherwise obtainable chance to learn:

1. The power of the press to help or to hurt;
2. The ways news can be managed and distorted;
3. The difficulties involved in the exercise of the freedom of the press;
4. The proper regard for taste and decency;
5. The great responsibilities of those who presume to inform, to persuade, to instruct, and to entertain and amuse;
6. The skills to read and listen intelligently;
7. Practical application of skills and knowledge acquired in other courses.

School and college newspapers appear in many forms, production processes, and schedules. Some yearbooks may be mimeographed and the photographs produced in the school darkroom. Large university newspapers may approach the public press in complexity and significance for their special readers. A weekly or a daily column or page in the local newspaper edited by students has many advantages, but it has not been widely used as a type of school newspaper.

Management. The management of publications requires dealing with the elements common to all human enterprises—the problems of staffing and staff organization, supervision, quality control, financing, and work facilities. As with each activity, there are special aspects of each element peculiar to publications.

Staffs are selected through election or appointment or some combination of the two. Generally, younger students start as third-level assistants—cub reporters—and work up to editorial responsibility of a special department or the publication as a whole. The existing staff is frequently the selecting body, for they are sure to know the students and the requirements of the different jobs. Only the editor-in-chief may be elected and given the responsibility for "hiring"—that is, for naming his chief assistants as business and advertising managers, editors of the social, sports, and feature columns, and the rest of the special workers.

The total staff includes most of the usual newspaper positions. These include feature, music, sports, book review editors, exchange and distribution managers, and columnists for such special columns as *Know Your Officers, Who's Who Among the New Faculty, Campus Capers, Our Seniors, Little Wheels.*

A thorny publication activity problem is the relation of the publication staff to the members and teachers of the journalism classes. Practice varies from systems in which the staff is composed entirely from students in the journalism courses with the teacher as newspaper advisor to those in which there is no formal relationship between the two. Between these extremes the two types of journalism activity are related in different degrees. The students in the course may, for example, put out one or a considerable number of issues of the newspaper as realistic practice experiences.

At the bottom is the old unsolved question of the relationship between the credit curriculum and the extracurriculum. This issue has been troublesome for as long as student activities and the credit system have existed. Theoretical positions vary as widely as does practice. The preferred position is that all student publication activities should be strictly noncredit. Students should not be restrained by any bylaws of the student constitution restricting staff appointments to students in credit courses.

The faculty advisor to student publications is, of course, a key person. He should have all the attributes and skills of a good teacher. In addition, he should be familiar with journalism. It is educationally unsound to assign as advisor a teacher with only the ordinary layman's knowledge of publishing. The activity is too important to put into unskilled hands; it imposes a burden which is professionally and personally unfair to an untrained person—and also unfair to students.

Student activities, as they reflect life outside the school, have grown in sophistication and complexity. Special preparation of the advisor is absolutely essential to insure that all the potential values of the publication experience will be derived by those directly involved, the school, the students, and the community as a whole. Some idea of the knowledge required by the advisor is suggested by the following list of related terms:

Glossary of Newspaper Terms

Add: An addition of late information to a story already written or in type.

Article: An informative discussion in expository form of news events or technical subjects.

Bank: A minor deck in a headline.

Banner: A headline in large letters extending across the top of the first page. (Also called a *streamer.*)

Boldface: Heavy black type. (Also called *blackface.*)

Boxed head: Headlines surrounded by rules.

Boxed summary: A summary of information (preceding a news article) enclosed by rules. Because the purpose is to give emphasis to certain points, the matter is usually set in boldface.

Breakover: Continuation of an article to another column or page; also the article itself.

Break page: The page on which stories are continued.

Bulletin: A brief telegraphic message giving merely the substance of an event without the details; often used to report accidents.

Clean copy: Copy that is free from errors.

Copy cutter: One who divides long news stories into several parts (called *takes*) to distribute to linotype operators. The purpose is to speed up the typesetting process.

Copyreader: One who edits copy to make it conform to the established style.

Cover: The process of getting the facts and writing up the report of a news event.

Deck: The divisions of a headline, usually separated from each other by dashes. (Also called *headline units.*)

Dirty copy: Copy that is full of errors.

Dope: Material to be used in a news story; used frequently in the sports department to refer to forecasts of the outcome of athletic contests.

Drophead: The headline below a banner or flag, referring to the flag story.

Drop line: A headline consisting of two, three, or four lines, each less than a column wide, descending like stair steps to the right.

Ears: Square boxes in the upper corners of the front page of a newspaper.

Em: A unit of measurement equal to the square of the height of any size or type.

En: A unit of measurement equal to half an em.

Font: A set of one size of type, containing capital letters, small letters, figures, punctuation marks, and spaces.

Hanging indentation: A headline in which the first line is set flush and the lines following are indented.

Jump: The line of division in a story that is continued to another page.

Lead story: The story placed in the right-hand column of the front page because it is the most important story in the issue.

Overset: Material in type that could not be run for lack of space.

Quality control. *Censorship* is a nasty word in a society which treasures free communication. The term *quality control* suggests a positive regard for excellence, good taste, and the rights and feelings of others. Surveillance by faculty advisors is gradually diminished as the students move from elementary school to college. Crises caused by major infractions of legal or extralegal mandates is to be avoided at all costs. This dictum of good practice suggests that prevention of such infractions is essential. A publishing code should be developed under the guidance of the publication board of the student council.[1] This code should be thoroughly understood by all involved in publication, especially by new staff members. The editors can then be trusted a long way.

Quality control is a broad term. It includes English usage, appearance, placement of important news, headlines, and all the other technical details of good journalism. It also includes the off-color

---

[1] Long before the Surgeon General's 1964 report on smoking and health was released, some publications refused cigarette ads. As early as 1963, American Tobacco, Lorillard, and other companies stopped advertising in college papers. In 1959, Frederick wrote in *The Third Curriculum, op. cit.,* p. 164: "No advertisement may be solicited . . . which promotes the sale of cigarettes, tobacco, beer, or wine. . . ." This is one of the four codes of advertising practice for school publications.

and offensive items that sometimes creep in, especially in the humor, social, and gossip columns.

When the editor of social news writes: "Guess who left a fraternity party Sunday at 3 AM barefoot up to her neck," harm may be done to the institution, to the girl, to the writer, and to journalism. The writer was probably being funny, not malicious; thus the point at issue is one of judgment. And the judgment of the young is faulty, precisely because it is young.

Prevention of such occurrences is to be preferred to crisis action —and such prevention requires planning and action before the fact. This is one of many good reasons why a trained and experienced advisor is so important to a student publication.

Colleges have a special problem in quality control, especially with respect to humor magazines. Practice varies from stultifying and stuffy censorship to complete freedom (except as the police may interfere). Only the very wealthy, long-established, private colleges can afford a policy of complete freedom.

Humor Magazine. The humor magazine has had little vogue in high schools. Some colleges do continue to lampoon or "put on the record." America, it is said, has lost the capacity to laugh at itself. If life is tragic, as some existentialists maintain, it is also comic. The therapy of laughter is needed now as always. Lincoln used humor to make serious points and, perhaps, to ease his burdens just a little. The right kind of humor should be encouraged in students, and it should be shared in publications. The risks, in terms of quality control, are great; but the values, in terms of relieving the pressures to which the younger generation is subjected, are even greater.

An analysis of student humor magazines showed that the jokes, in dialogue form, pertained to the following phases of student life:

Pinning	1	Cosmetic	1
Petting	28	Auto	3
Baldness	1	Puns	2
Nudity (female)	10	Marriage	2
Birth	2	Drink	3
Divorce	1	Dancing	2

The emphasis documents widely held conclusions respecting the nonwork interests of the young.

Student handbook.   The value of printing in the conduct of human enterprises is nowhere better illustrated than in the student handbook. If it is at all well done, it can be an ever-present help in time of need. It is a mine of information for both students and parents, and for anyone else interested in student activities. The elements included range from a list of important dates and curriculum offerings to codes of conduct for adolescents as devised by student-parent-teacher groups.

The yearbook.   In the opinion of many educators and parents, the process of producing the yearbook or annual has gotten completely out of hand. The cost in time and money is high. More and more juniors are included on the staff, for seniors are notably busy individuals. The useful life of this expensive history of the school year and the graduating class is short. Except for a very few sentimental persons and devoted alumni, the yearbook is relegated to a closet or a forgotten corner of the bookcase after a week or so. The publication experience is of a type with which very few of the students will be concerned as adults. The closest analogy to the yearbook that can be found in general publication is the annual report of a large corporation, which is prepared by professionals and read by a very select group of adults.

Nevertheless, the annual persists. It has been frozen into the activity program by tradition and sentiment. In the continuous reappraisal of education—and even in periods of intensive re-evaluation—no one has come up with a more acceptable or educationally sounder innovation.

Special Publications

Special publications (see page 24) are notably neglected in terms of utilization and quality control. They are frequently poorly done, and casually and carelessly used. Special homeroom, class, and special-interest publications and handbills are mimeographed—and, too often, scarcely readable. Bulletin boards are often messy and unattractive. News releases to the public press are frequently made by students and teachers with no editorial training and no guidance from an advisory board or commission on publications. The student-written weekly column of school news may be the result of a private arrangement between the student and a parent or friend on the local paper. Radio interviews with students who have received some honor or are publicizing some school event may or may not be used to best advantage. The use of motion pictures as a record of activities and as a means of communication is confined largely to athletics.

Speech

Introduction.   Free speech, free discussion, and free debate are the characteristics of western democracy. The ancient Greeks put a high value on speech and debate. The Romans followed suit. Cicero's orations were once very important in secondary school curriculums, and at one time every schoolboy was exposed to the speeches of Mark Antony, Shylock, Portia, Platonius, and Lincoln.

The origins of speech are lost in the dim recesses of human evolution. Man may be a rational animal because he speaks, or he may speak because he is a rational creature. All animals communicate through sounds or actions. The dog standing at the door and wagging his tail indicates he wants to be let out. It is, however, reserved to humans to form sounds into words and sentences to convey as well as to record information, to entertain, and to persuade.

Speech—formal or informal—is necessary for human societies. To the extent that schools and colleges prepare students for adult life by reflecting that life, speech training is a part of education. Recitations, reports, announcements, and speeches are a part of institutional life. Some of the speaking is informal, as when students discuss the desirability of supporting the proposal to require twenty units for a high school diploma. A smaller, but more noticeable part is formal, as when the students participate in debates, commencement orations, declamations, and interpretative reading.

Formal speech activities appeared early. In ancient Greece, skill in oratory and debate was highly prized. In "modern" times, speech became important in England as the English hammered out the basic tenets of modern democracy. A debate society was founded at Eton in 1811. At Exeter, a rhetorical society was organized in 1812 and the Phillips Club in 1841.

In recent decades speech activities have given ground to athletic and social events. The 1952 bulletin of the National Association of Secondary School Principals[2] did not consider speech and de-

---

[2] Gerald Van Pool, *Vitalizing Student Activities in the Secondary School,* Vol. 36, No. 184 (February 1952).

bating, perhaps because in many schools the activities have been moved into the elective curriculum and been made a part of the English courses. Miller, Moyer, and Patrick[3] treated speech under the title *Dramatics and Other Speech Activities.*

Speeches by men in public office have grown shorter—except, notably, in countries in which individual freedom is kept at a minimum level. In such countries two- or three-hour speeches are still common (and perhaps the persuasive effects of massed thousands of the faithful, and the trumpets, uniforms, banners, and other emotive devices are as important as the speeches). The decline of the long speech in the United States, England, and the other western democracies may be in part the result of the spread of television. It is clear that print and pictures have made the spoken word of less significance in public life. In the schools, where the senior oration was once the final requirement for graduation from college, now only the ranking scholars are required to make speeches. The doctoral candidate's public defense of his thesis is no longer universally required.

The activities in the credit and noncredit curriculums of democratic schools are wide in scope and varied in nature. That a very much larger percentage of students in high school and college do not participate in the more formal noncredit speech activities is to be regretted. It is not unusual to find graduate students who have never addressed an audience until required to present their theses. Medical men and engineers are notably poor speakers. Adult-education programs offer courses in public speaking to help successful men meet the requirements for reports and public appearances imposed by their elevations to positions of larger, broader, and more public responsibility.

Scope. The label *speech activities* covers a wide variety of activities, some of which are described below.

Corrective speech should properly be included in the student services division of American educational institutions. Attention to children and adolescents afflicted with stutters, aphasia, cleft palates, lazy lips, stage fright, and hearing blocks is more and more common.

Voice quality and diction have been the special concern of girls' finishing schools, but the value of well-modulated, well-trained

---

[3] F. A. Miller, J. H. Moyer, and R. B. Patrick, *Planning Student Activities* (Englewood Cliffs, N.J.: Prentice-Hall, Inc., 1956).

speech is increasingly recognized as a business asset as well as a social asset. Public schools rarely give systematic attention to the quality of normal speech except as teachers incidentally give advice and direction when students speak or read aloud in class or in the line of student government duties.

Conversation, polite or otherwise, is a universal occupation. The art of conversation is thought by some to be a lost art. Certainly, the loosening of tongues by martinis is not the educational answer. The slangy, cryptic "conversation" of the young is the despair of parents and teachers. At present, no systematic attention is given to this neglected and potentially most pleasant usage of the powers of human speech.

Discussion, both formal and informal, is mandatory in all societies. Such subjects as birth control, the population explosion, the chances of a bull market, the merits of foreign cars, or the effects of insecticides on the bees may be debated over bridge tables and in locker rooms. General discussion is not—and perhaps rightly so—the concern of teachers of speech. Formal discussions—as in panels, round tables, forums, and student council meetings—should be. There is a large body of literature on the role of the leaders and participants in such discussions. (Even the physical setup for a panel discussion is of importance. Nothing is worse than a panel where the participants cannot talk to one another because they do not face each other.)

Discussions inform, persuade, or convince—whether the topic be the school budget or the new patterns of social behavior among teenagers. Some school guidance and practice in discussion would be in keeping with the American philosophy of education as it was formulated before the advent of Sputnik I turned the United States to education as a weapon rather than as a way to a fuller life.

Public speaking—whether before a school assembly, a luncheon club, or a stockholders' meeting—is a special art. Some schools provide practice in this art, but few schools give much instruction to guide such practice. Public speaking is important and should be a part of the education of more Americans. Television and radio make important speech demands on those who speak before audiences. Every four years the national political conventions make public speaking a national pastime, or a national disgrace.

Oratory is another almost lost art—and perhaps properly so. The flowery rhetoric of a Douglas and a Bryan has yielded to the adroitness of a Roosevelt or a Lincoln and to the demands of the televised interview or panel discussion.

Declamation has had the same fate as oratory.

Extemporaneous (*extempore*) *speaking* is known largely by those involved in initiation ceremonies to learned societies, to doctoral degree candidates, and some professional fraternities. A few speech tournaments still include this event.

Interpretative reading is left to the teachers of English, although their training in this art is rarely stressed. Alexander Woollcott and Charles Laughton were among the last of the great exponents of reading as an aesthetic experience. Students in dramatics, however, still get considerable training and experience in this art.

Choral reading, or the verse choir, has a classical tradition in Greek drama. Such groups, however, are all too rare.

Storytelling survives in the elementary school's see-and-tell sessions. The raconteur is a rare and valuable person, now generally to be found only among the comic. Sam Levinson, for instance, follows in the tradition of the great Irving S. Cobb. The formation of storytelling clubs in schools and colleges might help to rescue the art from the perversion of the bar and cocktail party.

John Ciardi, in an article entitled "Tales and Tellers," wrote:[4]

A tale well told is an evening well spent and the art of story telling around the evening fireside was once a treasured part of home life. Movies, radio, the family car and now TV, have all but destroyed that art of the fireside, but it may yet be that recorded readings will do something to restore family listening.

Mr. Ciardi went on to review some new records of readings. Among these were: "Sir Michael Redgrave Reads Chekhov," "Roddy McDowell Reads the Horror Stories of H. P. Lovecraft," "Burgess Meredith reads Ray Bradbury," "Mark Twain Performed by Will Geer."

Perhaps these records and other electronic devices may revive interest in storytelling as they have revived interest in the opera.

Debate of the formal American variety has come to monopolize extracurricular speech activity. American scholastic debating has become organized, formalized, ritualized, and competitive. Debaters

---

4 "Tales and Tellers," *The Saturday Review,* November 16, 1963.

and their coaches have structured debating as a process. The relaxed, witty, informal, and sometimes sharp debates of the House of Commons under a Disraeli or a Churchill, and the urban debates of a Huxley, a Russell, or a Shaw are little known in America.

Scholastic debate is cast into a rigid mold: a proposition which may be national, statewide, or local; an affirmative and a negative case; main speeches and rebuttals; timekeepers and judges; and an official decision. Terms are defined; issues are agreed upon. Ten minutes each are allotted to the first constructive and negative speakers, the second constructive and negative speakers, and the first rebuttals, and five minutes for the second rebuttals and the summaries.

The judge or judges are guided by lists of directives and classified items. A sample is given below.

Debater _____ School _____ Position _____
Score _____

Maximum points allowed

20 *Knowledge of the question.* Does the debater show that he knows the subject through extensive reading?

15 *Analysis.* Does the debater understand the main issues? Does he see the issue in broad prespective?

15 *Organization.* Does the speaker have his material organized and in control?

10 *Evidence.* Does the debater use reasoning processes—induction, deduction, cause, analogy—well?

10 *Adaptation.* Does the debater adapt to the particular case of his opponents in constructive as well as rebuttal speech? Does he think during the debate or does he merely recite what he has memorized?

10 *Refutation and rebuttal.* Does the debater show effective skill in refuting the arguments of his opponents? Does he answer specific arguments or merely repeat his constructive material?

10 *Delivery.* Is the debater persuasive in presenting his material? Is his use of voice, timing, delivery, and emphasis effective?

10 *Teamwork.* Does the debater cooperate with his teammates by supporting and reinforcing their statements?

American school debate has its critics as well as its defenders. The critics deplore the competitive emphasis, the formality, the remoteness of the questions, and the restriction of participation to "star" debaters.

Suggestions for improvement are numerous. Among the proposals made are the following:

1. Extend the debating experience to more students in more intramural debates.
2. Use debate topics that are meaningful to the students and to the school community.
3. Increase the use of nondecision or informal audience decisions.
4. Use the single expert critic who can give an analysis and suggestions as well as a decision.
5. Decrease formality. Keep the stress on knowledge, analysis, mastery, and delivery, but put a higher premium on wit, ease, apt phrasing, and other such elements.

The dominance of debating in school speech activities is evidenced by the vast number of books and manuals on the subject, some of which are listed below:

Baird, Albert Craig, *Argumentation, Discussion and Debate.* New York: McGraw-Hill Book Company, 1950.

Braden, Waldo Warder, *Oral Decision Making; Principles of Discussion and Debate.* New York: Harper and Row, Publishers, 1955.

Courtney, Luther Weeks, *Practical Debating.* Philadelphia: J. B. Lippincott Co., 1949.

Howes, Raymond F., *Debating.* Boston: D. C. Heath & Company, 1931.

Hyslop, J. H., *Logic and Argument.* New York: Charles Scribner's Sons, 1908.

Potter, David, *Debating in the Colonial Chartered Colleges, 1862 to 1900.* New York: Teachers College, Columbia University, 1944.

Quimby, Brooks, *So You Want to Debate.* Portland, Me.: J. Weston Walch, 1954.

Phelps, Edith M., *Debaters Manual.* New York: H. W. Wilson Company, 1929.

CHAPTER IV

The Performing Arts

Dramatics

The history of dramatics is as old as man himself. Primitive man probably recounted his adventures in rhythmic chants and pantomime. Ancient peoples practiced religious rites in dramatic forms. Masks were used to hide identities and to preserve illusions. Intense emotions were expressed through pantomimes, chants, and dances.

The theater is older than schools and colleges as these are known in the Western world. It is through the records of the ancient Greeks that we first learn of the arts of the actor and the playwright. Aeschylus, Sophocles, Euripedes, Aristophanes and their works form an important part of the human heritage. And, later, Shakespeare was to make his great contribution to our knowledge of Western man.

Since early times, dramatics have been participated in by young people and have been considered a valuable part of their education. Dramatics may have first been introduced into the schools in the Middle Ages. In the church schools of this period, the choir boys were also actors. In Elizabethan London, the choir boys at St. Paul's Cathedral took part in many religious dramas. Because women of virtue were not allowed on the stage, young boys played female parts.

Terry[1] noted that "Queen Elizabeth ordered the headmaster of Westminster to have a Latin play acted each year at Christmas to help the boys spend the holidays more profitably and to encourage them in graceful gesture and pronunciation."

Dramatic activities take many forms, are used by different groups, and are presented in different media. Churches present

---

[1] P. W. Terry, *Supervising Extracurricular Activities in the American Secondary School* (New York: McGraw-Hill Book Company, 1930). Note how frequently student activities appeared first in England, not on the Continent.

articles of faith in dramatic form and also put on plays to raise money. Community theaters provide recreational activities for many adults. Some of these groups have attained wide recognition.

Schools use dramatic forms as part of the instructional and recreational program. Elementary school children "play store." In the upper elementary grades and in the junior and senior high schools, dramatics are among the more popular student activities. The senior play is a fixture in many high schools. Drama clubs are almost universal. Plays written for college production are sometimes brought to Broadway.

Drama, like many other aspects of human culture represented in education, is part of the credit curriculum as well as of the noncredit curriculum. Dramatic forms are studied as literature and are used as methodological instruments in many subjects from the kindergarten to the graduate school. Then, of course, there are courses in dramatic arts for professionals and serious amateurs. Independent schools of dramatic arts are numerous, and higher institutions have departments of dramatic arts for undergraduates and graduate students.

Every human mystery, difficulty, problem, and danger provides subject matter for the dramatist. Man's joys and sorrows, his hopes and frustrations, and his successes and failures find their way to the play script, if not always to the stage. Truly is all the world a stage, and all persons actors on it.

The forms by which life is represented dramatically include:

1. Pantomime
2. Proscenium (conventional)
3. Arenas (circle in the round)
4. Pageants
5. Role-playing (casual)
6. Circuses
7. Puppets
8. Marionettes
9. Social drama (structured)
10. Skits
11. Tableaux

Each of these forms may be varied almost infinitely.

There may be "magic" in the theater, but there is also a lot of work. The wide scope of dramatic activities is suggested by the varied skills and processes which are employed in the production of a play for public presentation. Each of the following is, of course, a complex of knowledges, skills, and personality traits. Play production involves:

1. Selection
2. Casting
3. Costuming
4. Stage design
5. Stagecraft
6. Props
7. Make-up
8. Directing
9. Acting
10. Prompting
11. Reviewing
12. Business management
13. Program design
14. Crowd management
15. Ushering
16. Promotion
17. Publicity
18. Lighting
19. Playwriting
20. Safety control
21. Watching

Festivals, conferences, workshops, after-the-play parties, and rehearsals add to the range of experiences possible in dramatic activities. No other enterprise has the scope of dramatics, precisely because drama is as broad as life itself.

Theater provides an outlet for and a direct use of knowledges and skills acquired in almost every subject in the curriculum from typing class to the electrical shop. Music, dance, literature, history, bookkeeping, and public speaking are all used. Drama is an important—if not in fact the most important—activity in providing an immediate use for learnings acquired in the credit curriculum. The scope of drama suggests that the benefits to participants and consumers can be as wide as life's values. Important knowledges, skills, and attitudes are learned through participation in dramatic activities. Punctuality, dependability, concentration, poise, and many other qualities are required and practiced. Even research as a scholarly endeavor may be necessary, for interpretation of a role may be aided by digging into an historic period or the psychology of a character.

Specific values to individuals commonly allocated to dramatics are listed in a variety of ways. Among these are:

1. Artistic discrimination
2. Poise
3. Gracefulness
4. Emotional balance
5. Integration of personality
6. Creativity

All the social objectives of education so much stressed in American education may, in fact, be reached through direct practice in dramatic activities. The worthy use of leisure, health, and citizenship may be reinforced by dramatic coaches.

Practical values to the institution must be mentioned, for these values loom large—too large, sometimes. Plays can be used to raise money, to advertise the school or college, to attract new students, and to promote careers of those concerned. That these values should be secondary is emphasized by most educators. It should be noted and emphasized that making money is not evil, nor is ambition, rightly restrained, sinful. Only the sacrifice of higher values for the sake of box office success or personal ambition is to be condemned.

Music

Music, a part of human history. Music has been a part of all human history. Every human culture has had some kind of music. Man has used music to express his feelings, his hopes, his troubles, and his joys. In music can be read the character of a people and of an age. At times, the simplicity of the one-two-three of the waltz is enjoyed. At other times, only the fury of the atonal, diatonic idiom will express the inner confusion men feel.

Transistor radios, television, tapes, and records have put music on the beach, in the stadium stands, on the street, and in every room in the house including the bedroom and the study. Listeners are made in transistorized America, where consumption is easier than production. Listening is not entirely passive; it is active in special ways. The sale of recordings and instruments is phenomenal. What its long-range effects on musical interests and tastes will be is debatable. It is a fact that the audience for opera has increased each year, and that more symphony orchestras are playing than ever before.

What seems to have been a cultural explosion in America in the post-World War II era has not greatly influenced the schools and colleges. For most students, from elementary school to graduate school, music is still very incidental. The space age drive for excellence was a response to the survival-defense syndrome. The almost complete neglect of music (except of the marching band variety) as a participating experience for the many would appear to suggest that those prescribing and distributing funds for education saw little more to national life than industrial, scientific, and military strength. The late President Kennedy did start to bring culture to Washington, and New York City did build a center for the performing arts. But American students, for the most part, were encouraged or driven by defense-minded leaders to academic pursuits and muscle-building activities, not to the cultivation of musical interests and skills.

The Biennial Survey of Education of the U.S. Office of Education, in its review of subject enrollments in the high schools, had no entry for music until 1915; but in that year 31.5 per cent of the pupils enrolled were studying music of some kind. Comparable percentages were:

	Music	Art	Physical Education
1922	25.3	14.7	5.7
1928	26	11.7	15.0
1934	25.5	8.7	50.7
1949	30.1	9.0	69.4

Music did not benefit from state laws similar to those which mandated physical education. Perhaps, the word *benefit* is wrong, for those junior high schools that have established required music courses have not regarded the experiment as markedly successful.

Music and—to a greater degree—drama, painting, sculpture, and dancing are by their very nature best done by professionals. Most persons find their only contact with the arts will be in the role of "consumers." Music may, and perhaps should, deliberately be made an exception to this rule. This is meant to suggest that the schools and colleges should give higher priority to the encouragement of music activities for all students.

Aims of activities in music.   A special word has to be said about the aims of music activities. They are, of course, both general and vocational. Vocational aims are properly a part of the credit curriculum leading to a diploma. In the noncredit activities, the general aim of *enjoyment* should be stressed. *Stress* is the proper word, for of course, no complete separation of the vocational and the general is possible.

The general aims include all the values mankind has ever found in music. There is no reason to list a great many specific objectives. There is a fair amount of nonsense in saying and thinking that music "builds" ethical character, sobriety, morality, good citizenship, sound health, and all the rest of the human values. To say that "every patriotic emotion is aroused through the common touch of music" is completely ridiculous. Music can be used to help sell war bonds, or to ease the pain of the final farewell to a loved one. It can promote family solidarity, or set a religious atmosphere. At best, music—as a part of general education—is to be *enjoyed*.

The vocational aim of a music program is nothing more or less than to so train those who pursue the course sequence that they can earn a living or add to their income through musical activities—whether these be composing, singing, or teaching.

This division of aims into general and vocational suggests a way out of the thorny question of which music activities should be curricular or extracurricular. Those elements of music education designed to contribute to serious vocational skills should be part of the credit curriculum. In credit courses, marks should be based on the student's success in acquiring salable skills and knowledges. The practice of giving diploma credit as a way of forcing attendance at band rehearsals, or insuring the graduation of a weak student degrades the validity of credits and subverts the values of music.

The National Association of Secondary School Principals approved list of contests for 1958–59 did not include a single one in music. Livestock judging and soap sculpture were on the list, but not one musical activity. It is, however, true that competitiveness in music has considerable appeal and that this appeal is growing. Music contests, festivals, and tournaments have been developed on a large scale. The traditional order of judgments— first, second, third—has to an encouraging extent given way to broad-range quality ratings. If this trend continues, then such competitions will serve highly desirable educational purposes. Music should not be made to rely on extrinsic motivation. Rigid methods of selection, high-pressure drives, and large spectacles should not be allowed to replace music for the sake of music.

But no neglect of quality should be inferred from these statements. Learning to enjoy the competent performance of a musical selection is valuable and—to most persons—pleasurable. The casual "anything goes" attitude is acceptable at times. There are also times when excellence should be the only goal.

The use of the students' performance in contests as a measure of the quality of the teaching of the music faculty is as reprehensible as using the size of gate receipts at athletic events to measure the quality of teaching in the physical education department. Without reference to the time and cost involved in these contests, the abilities of students from different schools, or any other of the many factors involved, it is clear that—in the realm of music—competition, feuds, and quality "labels" have no place. The desire to do better, to get more enjoyment, and to give more pleasure is a higher motive than the wish to beat somebody else.

The values of music need no extended repetition here. The great church hymns, the massive national anthems, the long tradition of military bands and bugles, the popularity of political campaign songs, and recently the soothing musical background in industrial plants make clear that, in all his endeavors, man has sought the inspiration and the solace of music. The road may bend, and the day may end without a song; but all roads and all days are made richer or more bearable with music.

Scope. The scope of musical activities in schools and colleges is very wide, ranging from the elaborate college production of an original musical show or Broadway hit to the kindergarten rhythm band. No institution (except perhaps the very largest universities) will at any one time have groups involved in all the possible forms of music and associated music activities. The large, highly visible elements—marching band, chorus, and orchestra—dominate the program in most schools. These activities, unfortunately, have less chance of being carried over into adult life. Small instrumental or choral ensembles of various types should be more widely used, but the pull of the spectacular is very strong.

The following list, though partial, will suggest the scope of possible musical activities.

Instrumental:

1. Instruction
2. Rhythm band
3. Orchestra
4. Brass choir
5. String ensemble
6. Percussion ensemble
7. Pep band
8. Marching band
9. Stage band
10. Twirling
11. Flag swing
12. Dance band

Vocal:

1. Instruction
2. Choral
3. *A capella* choir
4. Glee club
5. Madrigal group
6. Choral speaking

7. Operetta
8. Musical festival
9. Musical play
10. Quartets
11. Sextets

Special:

1. Hi-fi club
2. Record club
3. Appreciation classes
4. Music festival
5. Opera appreciation
6. Disc jockey show

7. Assembly
8. Half-time show
9. School organ
10. Dining room music
11. Summer music camp

As with all human capacities, musical talent is distributed over a wide range. Relatively few persons lack all capacity for musical expression in any form, and even fewer have the musical genius of a Wagner or a Mozart. Quite naturally, music instructors and directors seek out the able students for their performing groups. Depending on the number of students and the school's music facilities and educational philosophy, opportunities to participate may also be available for those students who fall in the lower reaches of the scale of ability. Several things are suggested by these facts. More attention to large-group singing—as in assemblies, at commencement, and at athletic events—would appear desirable. Part-singing could be developed and attention focused on attack, phrasing, and clarity of pronunciation.

The musically gifted students, though much below the genius level, will generally be interested in music. They will get the solo parts, be made student directors, and participate widely in music activities of all kinds. Some procedures for encouraging practice in composing, arranging, and orchestration as part of course work or as a serious hobby in a club could be made.

Music could be instituted as a major sequence in the credit curriculum more widely than is the case now. Minors in music might well be encouraged on the college level. Encouragement rather than discouragement should be the policy respecting continuing private music lessons through high school and college. Too many young people with real ability find they have to give up their music because of the pressure of other school-imposed duties and activities. Public recognition of musical accomplishment is not nearly as common as is recognition of athletic or scientific accomplishments.

Dance

Dancing, like drama and music, is as old as man himself. The forms have differed, but the essential elements remain the same: motion and rhythm. Dancing is associated with every human experience: birth, death, joy, grief, religion, sex, thirst, hunger, war, peace—all have been celebrated or expressed in dancing.

The harvest, snake, rain, war dances of the American Indians are part of every American schoolboy's lore. Strange and tragic is our tendency to make jokes of these dances and of those of older cultures; but the sacred rituals of one era often become the superstitions of another. Progress can be cruel as well as meliorative.

Dancing was recognized by the early colonists. In 1625 the Reverend John Cotton said:[2]

Dancing (yea though mixt) I would not simply condemn. For I see two sorts of mixed dancings in use with God's people in the Old Testament, the one religious, Exod XV, 20, 21, the other civil, tending to the praise of conquerors, as the former of God, I Sam. XVII, 6, 7. Only lascivious dancing to wanton ditties, and amorous gestures and wanton dalliances, especially after feasts, I would bear witness against, as a great *flabella libidinis.*

Dancing has long been a part of Western education. Joseph Marks III reported that John Milton had mentioned dance in his *Tractate On Education* (1644). John Locke in *Some Thoughts Concerning Education* (1690) suggested that children "should be taught dance as soon as they are capable of learning it. Dancing being that which gives graceful Motions all the life and above all things Manliness and a becoming Confidence to young Children, I think cannot be learned too early. . . ."[3]

The dance has been neglected in American education. The elementary schools have made some use of the folk-dance and the Maypole for special purposes as auditorium programs for parents; but no really serious use of the dance as a part of education has ap-

---

[2] Quoted by Joseph Marks III, *America Learns To Dance* (New York: Exposition Press, 1957), p. 17.

[3] Quoted by Joseph Marks III, *op. cit.,* p. 15.

peared. Square-dancing and country-dancing have sometimes been encouraged, but the dance in general has yielded to the emphasis on games, sports, and social events. It is difficult, if not impossible, to get a group of teen-age boys to put on white tie and tails and dance with girls on the stage for an *entr'acte* at the spring music festival. Dance as an art form has all but disappeared, except perhaps on television.

The situation is not much different in college. Ted Shawn and Isadora Duncan founded the Denishawn School. Their tours carried the dance to many college campuses. In 1933, after a teaching hitch at the Springfield College, Shawn formed his all-male dance team, which appeared before many college audiences. But it was a spectator event.

Dance—tap, acrobatic, interpretative, formal and modern—is taught in some colleges as part of the credit curriculum. Dance appears as a part of student activities, but only incidentally (as in musical shows).

The fact is, of course, that in American education *dance* has come to mean ballroom dancing. A notable exception is in the physical education programs as conducted by some instructors. They have taken dancing over and introduced many American students to the possibilities of something other than dancing as a heterosexual enterprise. Future teachers of physical education probably get more dance instruction than any other group.

The theory that dance rather than dancing should be encouraged as a student activity and made part of the credit curriculum is a debatable one. The arts—particularly the performing arts—cannot be forced on the student.[4] America is, and has been, committed to active, productive endeavors. There is no time to stop at a crossroads and dance in the moonlight, or to express religious ecstasy or joy or sadness by the dance. There is no continental American counterpart to the sit-down hula of Hawaii. (With Westernization, even the hula has become a tourist spectacle.) The ballet has enjoyed a revival as a performing art, but not as yet as a student activity. That the physical education teachers can do very much is doubtful.

---

[4] It is interesting to note that on December 15, 1963, the Ford Foundation announced it had made grants of $7,756,750 to eight organizations to further the development of professional ballet in the United States over a ten-year period. *The New York Times,* December 16, 1963.

The outlook for the performing arts will not brighten as long as scientific pursuits have top priority.

Nevertheless, the programs of some colleges and universities are well known, for they are offered to the general public in the same way, if not to the same extent, as are football and basketball.[5] (Less generally known is the work of the secondary schools.) The scope of drama as a college-level activity was dramatically presented at a testimonial dinner for the Reverend Gilbert V. Hartke, who has headed the drama department of Catholic University since its establishment in 1937.[6]

In twenty-five years the department has produced more than two hundred plays and musicals. Of these, forty-one were original productions of students and faculty. The University Players were founded in 1949. A subgroup, The National Players, is a touring company which travels across the country and visits American military bases overseas. A feature of the University Players is a summer stock company at Onley, Maryland, and a summer theater at Winooski, Vermont.

The dinner marked the opening of a campaign to raise funds for a six-hundred-seat theater, a two-hundred-seat laboratory theater, a rehearsal hall, dressing rooms, a library, and offices for the faculty.

Some notion of the place of drama and music in the activity program of the American secondary schools may be conveyed by reference to the work of the schools in Kansas. Under the leadership of the Kansas State High School Activities Association, the performing arts—especially drama and interpretative reading—have been given a large place in the lives of the youth of Kansas.

Under the rules and regulations established by the association, district and statewide festivals are held. The choice of the term *festivals* rather than *competitions* is a significant one. Behind these festivals are literally thousands of experiences in dramatics, music, and speech. For thousands of students, the festivals are means of encouragement, recognition, and improvement; not a tooth-and-claw competition for formal honors.

---

[5] Courses in the arts are rarely listed as basic college entrance requirements. The National Council of the Arts In Education is a federation representing teachers in art, architecture, dance, music, and the theater arts at all levels of education.

[6] *The New York Times,* April 28, 1963.

CHAPTER V

Social Activities

Introduction. There is probably no more controversial area in the total life of the students than that vague domain called *social.* All children and their parents are concerned, either because they are wholesomely involved, or because they are dangerously involved, or because they are not involved at all. All teachers are concerned, because in one way or another, they will be called upon to participate by chaperoning, by attending or by involving themselves in planning social affairs. Parents are completely baffled by the changed patterns of social life of the young.

The term social. The professional literature on school social activities of youth reveals the still unresolved conflict of the school's role in such activities. The frank recognition that educational institutions in America have been thrust into the business of providing for, managing, and regulating much of the social life of the young is difficult even for educators to make. The school's role in the religious life of the young is dealt with in the Constitution and is subject to judicial review. The social life is left without benefit of legal guidance.

Social, in the present context, includes all the meetings of persons "just for fun." People may come together by twos, by fours, or by the hundreds or thousands, but the object is always the pleasure of human contact. The purpose or excuse for such meetings may be bridge, cocktails, food, dancing, courtship, movies, or anything else; but the aim is for people to enjoy people. When a book company or a jewelry manufacturer throws a party at a school principals' convention, the purpose is to sell a product. It is primarily a business activity. When the young executive entertains the boss, he hopes to further his own career. He and the boss might possibly be "purely" socializing, but the odds are against it. This the boss very likely understands. Social is noninstrumental at the conscious level.

All activities in which people engage primarily to enjoy other people are social. The motive dominating the act determines the character of the act and the proper use of the term *social*. The educator's dilemma is caused by the fact that with most normal humans between the ages of twelve and one hundred, the most enjoyable portion of the human race is the opposite sex. There are certainly exceptions: men do go on fishing trips with other men, and women do have their afternoon bridge clubs. But the sailors in *South Pacific* stated the general rule in their "There Is Nothing Like a Dame." Underlining this point is the story about Will Rogers, who was asked to a banquet to say a few words. He did, and later sent the group a bill for $1,000. Outraged, the group reminded him that the invitation had been social. He replied, "When I am invited out socially Mrs. Rogers is invited too."

As with all human activities and motivations, nothing is ever pure. Motives are almost always mixed. The love of music draws people to the concert halls, but the audience is usually made up of couples. Most people apparently enjoy the concert more with a member of the opposite sex. An all-boy dance is unthinkable; an all-girl dance isn't worthwhile.

The schools' role in guiding or guarding the heterosexual development of the youth of the land has not yet been accepted as theory, though it has been forced on them in fact. The literature is filled with discussions of dating practices, codes of conduct, sexual practices, mixed entertainment in resident halls, and a host of related topics. College presidents have been moved to explain what the catalogue requirement of "high moral standards" means.

This social responsibility of schools and colleges is typically American. The European universities and secondary schools have very little concern for anything except the intellectual development of students, although there are faint signs of an educational "reform." The American problem arises from the central role of the school in American life and the relatively lesser place accorded the home and the church. This story has been told many times. It is clear that American educational institutions have a part in dances, balls, teas, hayrides, pre- and post-football parties, commencement activities, and many other affairs.

Varieties of Activities

Social activities range from a stroll across the campus to a formal ball with corsages, favors, programs, and a big-name orchestra. A list of social activities would be endless, for the outings, dances, parties, and picnics are as varied as the human imagination. Eating events include formal banquets, snacks, a coke at the local drugstore, or a congenial lunch in the school dining room. Receptions and informal teas would have to be included. When two or more people get together to enjoy each other in any way, a social activity has taken place.

Of special importance are what might be called activities of deliberate instruction. These go under a variety of names, often chosen to disguise their real function. "Subdeb" clubs, "social grace" clubs, "valet" clubs, for example, are formed to consider selection and care of clothes; use of cosmetics; good posture; weight control; hair styling and care; acceptable ways of attracting favorable notice; ways of asking for, accepting, or refusing dates; proper care and feeding of chaperones; proper conduct; moral standards; manners; and all other elements in informal associational living.

A few institutions have established courses in sex, marriage and family life; but as Herbert Spencer pointed out long ago, an examination of the textbooks and syllabi of our schools and colleges would lead future historians to conclude that these schools were designed for celibates. Sex education is still not considered "proper" education for the young—or, at least, not proper for schools and colleges. The matter is left to friends, parents, fraternity brothers, and books (which were, until recently, hard to find).

The major official concern of institutional authorities has been supervision, regulation, control—and punishment after the fact. The official attitude has been a negative one, except in the provision of attractive facilities for dining and for all forms of social activity, including sports and games, dances, boating, riding, and hiking.

Some schools, however, do take a positive stand in fostering the kinds of special clubs mentioned above. Others have developed homeroom discussion guides which consider among other things, the teaching of junior high school boys to enjoy dancing rather than horseplay, and the teaching of all students to write thank-you notes, to make and accept introductions, and to treat parents with proper respect.

Values

The values which could be achieved through expert management of social activities in the school and in the home are nothing short of richly rewarding in all their many phases. Social activities serve to transform the awkward, shy, boisterous, and crude youngster into a relaxed, knowledgeable, skillful, and attractive adult who is a good companion, a sensitive lover, and a satisfying partner in marriage.

The millennium, of course, is not around the corner. Besides the reluctance and the lack of vision or courage on the part of school authorities to do the job in a straightforward manner, there are inevitable limitations on their effectiveness. Early conditioning is always a factor. Parents, as well as teachers, are not equipped to do an adequate "socializing" job even when they have the vision and courage to try. The responsibility is tossed back and forth among the several institutions, and that responsibility is the most critical of all relationships. Even the newspapers get into the act with their various "advice" columns.

Then, too, all individuals have some physical and psychological handicaps. Pimples, glasses, obesity, overanxiety, aggressive intelligence, and a thousand other real and imagined defects block easy and natural socializing. The schools have not—and perhaps cannot —cope with all these things.

Among the attitudes that are approved, and in varying degrees developed by schools and colleges are courtesy, good manners, and consideration and respect for the rights and feelings of others.[1] A sense of responsibility for the pleasure, the needs, and the wishes of others is universally emphasized. Teachers have, in thousands of real situations, put the weight of their influence on the side of the right, the nice, the proper thing to do and say.

The social skills of the livingroom, the ballroom, and the playing field are a constant concern to educators. Youngsters are taught— though generally incidentally—many of the social how-to's: how

---

[1] *The New York Times* (February 2, 1964) reported that some school clubs in the Soviet Union were instructing in table manners, how to set a table and serve a meal, good grooming, morality, dress, and behavior in public.

to ask for, accept, or refuse a date and a dance; how to make introductions; how to give and acknowledge compliments and honors; how to win or lose a game; how to dance and play bridge, golf, and tennis; how to sail a boat; how to scull a punt; how to order a meal and pay the check; how to introduce a speaker, and on and on.

These attitudes and skills are not trivial. Knowing how to seat a group at the dinner table, how to dress for an all-day picnic, or how to go through a receiving line may not add much to the national defense, but such knowledge does contribute enormously to human happiness. As any rejected teen-ager can testify, it is people who make us happy or sad. Getting along with people depends on having the proper social skills and attitudes.

The fact that these and other attitudes and skills are not embodied in approved courses of study must not be taken as an indication that they are not valuable. Present theories on how accepted attitudes and skills can best be taught, where, when, and by whom are based only on experience. Perhaps experience is the best basis —although thousands of teachers who chaperone eighth-grade parties would welcome formal guidelines to the making of gracious ladies and courtly gentlemen.

Management

Educational authorities are quite properly, and by necessity, concerned with the management of social activities. The emphasis is still almost exclusively on regulation and control: order, system, regularity, physical safety, and the good reputation of the institution are the primary concerns. The opportunities to teach attitudes and skills are less subject to deliberate planning and less dominant in the general thinking of school principals.

Organized activities include all the affairs held under the aegis of the institution. They must be planned, conducted, reported on, evaluated, and used as the basis for suggestions for future guidance.

The elements which must be handled are numerous. Students must be taught to deal with cost, guests, chaperones, party crashers, drinking, smoking, publicity, lighting, official curfews, transportation, clean-up, evaluation, parking, use of public buildings, police services, and other details.

Planning procedures and their value are taught through social activities in a natural situation. Chairmen are taught to delegate responsibility and to evaluate the performance of their assistants. A school dance, for example, is a complex affair. Official permission must be obtained and the affair must be scheduled and registered. The following form is a composite of several in general use:

REQUEST FOR APPROVAL OF PARTY OR DANCE

Group sponsoring ....

Who may attend ....

Date ....

Hour beginning .... ending ....

General chairman ....

Chairmen of other committees ....
....

Names of chaperones ....

    Parents ....
....

    Faculty ....

Signatures of faculty sponsors ....
....

Items of expense ....
....

Total expense ....

Plan for meeting expense ....
....

Entertainment at party ....
....

Date of application for permit ....

Room reservation ....

Plans approved by ....
....

Date approved ....

Social Board of Student Council

The chairman and the dance committee must attend to many of the details that make a dance possible and enjoyable. The memo below is a general reminder to planning committees.

TO CHAIRMAN AND DANCE COMMITTEE MEMBERS

1. Get name and theme for dance.
2. Assign committee members to handle the following:
    A. Orchestra

      B. Tickets: printing, sale
      C. Programs
      D. Decorations
      E. Prizes (if any)
      F. School and newspaper publicity
      G. Entertainment at intermission
      H. Chaperones
      I. Refreshments
      J. Clean-up (arrange for ten boys to help after the dance)
      K. Custodians

3. Work with all committees.
4. Find out about:
      A. Ice cream
      B. Corn meal or wax on floor?
      C. Janitors on duty
      D. Leads and lamps for special lighting effects
      E. Public address system
      F. Place for wraps, checkers on duty, fee (if any)

5. Have two people on the door, and be sure one is there during intermission. Also, must have at least five people to handle posts: two at west door from 7:30 PM to close of dance, one at north door, one inside, and one for general supervision of corridors.

6. Lock all doors in building including faculty rooms and lavatories.

7. Open lavatories on first floor only.

8. Have one teacher in charge of the sale or dispensing of refreshments.

9. This is a private dance: sell no tickets at the door; admit no non-students.

10. Dress: not formal, but as for church.

11. Invite parents and guardians to attend as guests.

12. Serve all refreshments in the cafeteria.

13. Get announcer for public address system.

14. Get check made out to pay for orchestra in advance.

15. Remove all decorations right after the dance.

16. Provide instruction in dancing for those who do not dance.

17. Be sure all faculty committee members are present at the dance.

18. If tickets are taxable, students who receive free tickets must pay the tax on them.

19. Parking: police or custodians; check highway entrance to campus.

20. Make out a financial report for the principal and the student council. Obtain from all chairmen a list of expenses, and make a duplicate of final report.

21. Fill out evaluation and suggestion report.

NOTE: If there is to be square dancing at the dance make sure that arrangements have been made for a caller. Check all the above items with the social board.

Control or reminder forms have been developed for other types of social activities. A dance has been used here because it is the most popular social activity.

The Problem

With the changes in patterns of life following the Great Depression, the two world wars, and the emancipation of women, educational authorities and parents have discovered new problems of management.

A standard joke of the decade is that the college president has three major problems: building athletic teams for the alumni and the publicity department, providing parking space for the faculty, and restraining the sex drive of the undergraduates.[2] To harassed presidents, school superintendents, and principals, to busy police chiefs, and to baffled parents, early marriages, steady dating, dormitory entertainments, pregnant students, vague rumors of sex clubs and amorous activities on the campus and in the school are not jokes but realities. And one evidence of the reality of the problem is the rise in the incidence of venereal disease among high school and college students.

Social, to the adolescent, means the opposite sex. Sex is no longer the exclusive pastime of the fast set, the dilettanti at Nice and Cannes, or the country club set. Urbanization, mass communication, and science have seen to that. Kinsey, Ford and Beach, Miller, Baldwin, Williams, Salinger, O'Neill, and the others have looked behind or under romance. Freud, *Lolita, Playboy,* the old *Esquire,* and the undergarment and deodorant ads have stripped many of the illusions, and much of the gallantry from boy-girl relationships. It is literally true that nothing is now unmentionable in mixed company.

Behind the fun and the notable values of social activities lies a problem of unrealized dimensions. Between the ages of thirteen

---

[2] One branch of the National Union of Teachers in England took the position that the schools should do something to develop high moral and social standards. The modern school section took the position that such guidance should not be thrust on the schools.

and nineteen, and perhaps earlier, boys and girls begin to date, dance, and—more and more frequently—to drink. Sex has accompanied these pastimes, invading the high school and is slipping even into the junior high school.

The problem is now serious for girls as well as boys. One anecdote tells of Mother and Dad watching their son leave for his first dance date. They gave the usual advice, including, "Boys respect a girl's 'No.' " "But Mother," said the boy, "what if she doesn't say 'No'?" As early as 1951, *Time* could say in a report on American youth:

American young women are in many ways the generation's most serious problem. . . . They were raised to believe in woman's emancipation and equality with man. . . . There is every evidence that they have not been made happy by their ascent to power. . . .

To prove that the younger generation can still raise hell, *Time* reported that at a party for a flunked-out coed:

The tipsy blond ripped the big tackle's shirt from his shoulders and staggered off through the crowded room fan dancing with a ragged sleeve. In her wake shirts fell in shreds on the floor, until half the male guests were bare to the waists. . . . In one corner four tipsily solicitous coeds tried to revive a passed-out couple with more red dog. . . . At 2 AM when the party broke up, one car load of youngsters decided to take off on a two-day drive into Mexico.

Neither the fine suburban schools nor the venerated Ivy League colleges and universities are immune from this change in patterns of sexual relationships. The old, old question—What is our younger generation coming to?—is raised anew, but as with each generation, in a new dimension. Almost half of all American women marry before the college graduation age. More and more high schools permit the attendance of married students, and some even permit pregnant girls to walk in the graduation procession.

The elementary schools are experiencing the downward thrust of adult patterns into childhood years. Nine-year-olds are beginning to date and twelve-year-olds are going steady. Mothers buy "training bras" and garter belts and nylons for nine-year-old girls. Some eight-year-olds are treated to twenty-five-dollar permanents. *The New York Herald-Tribune* reported that "some of the 26 AA size bras are padded for little girls with an inferiority complex."

Broderick and Fowler[3] reported, in *New Patterns of Relationship Between the Sexes Among Pre-Adolescents,* that the old childhood antagonisms were disappearing. The data, they said, were "impressive." Among fifth-grade boys, 86.8 per cent admit they "have a sweetheart," 68.1 per cent say the sweetheart knows, 63.7 per cent say their friends know, and 62.0 per cent say their parents know; 45 per cent have dated, 72.7 per cent have been kissed, and 79.5 per cent admitted or bragged that they had kissed girls; 35 per cent preferred to eat with girls, 49.0 per cent preferred to go walking with girls, and 58.5 per cent preferred to go to the movies with girls. Fifth-grade boys are about ten or eleven years old. The investigators concluded in what will be to some parents a too-scientific understatement: "While old patterns of hostility and withdrawal are not dead, new behavior and relationships are developing."

College authorities are bedeviled by the drive for undergraduate privacy. Because cars offer a way to find privacy, undergraduates want a relaxation of the rules against having cars. As one frankly states, it is more important that the cars have doors than that they have wheels. Dormitory visiting hours, "late-out" privileges, off-campus weekends, "semiprivate" social space, and mixed entertainment in residence halls are all being demanded—and they are being conceded, however grudgingly.

The New York Times reported that "Columbia College boys will be allowed to entertain female guests in their dormitory rooms on alternate Sundays from two to five provided the doors are kept open." The definition of *open* was debated, and finally determined to be "the width of a book." Of course, there are many "books," including a book of matches.

The social problem is obviously not a male monopoly. Fall weekends, winter carnivals, boating days make more complicated President Blanding's dictum at Vassar's 1962 opening convocation that if students wished to indulge in premarital sex relations or *excessive* drinking they must resign from the college. It is clear that worried parents who want to protect their daughters can find no comfort in sending them to a woman's college or to an all-

[3] C. B. Broderick and S. E. Fowler, *Marriage and Family Living 1961,* Vol. 23 (1961), 27–30. Also in J. E. Seidman, *Education for Mental Health* (New York: Thomas Y. Crowell Company, 1963).

girls school. The automobile has destroyed the sex-segregated college and the separate boys' and girls' secondary schools.

Symptoms, Causes, and Effects

Symptoms, causes, and effects are always difficult to unravel. What has caused the well-documented changes in boy-girl relationships? The list of preferred causes is long and controversial. It is difficult to separate primary or basic causes from secondary or immediate causes; and causality is, of course, one of science's unsolved problems. The general insecurity of the post-World War II area no doubt lies at the base of much that bedevils responsible citizens of the world. About these, educationists can do little directly—which may suggest that Americans have lost faith in education as a way to peace, security, quietude, and a good life.

To retreat from the general questions of the human predicament in an absurd existence to the immediate and obvious is, if not intellectually sound, of more direct concern to those who are charged with the social activities of the young. In this mood the following factors can be listed as "causes":

1. Exposure to sex occurs earlier. Homes are small; walls are thin; apartments are close together. Small homes keep the youngsters in the same bed or the same room too long. Advertisements leave nothing to the imagination—nor do styles of dress and sweaters or the jokes of television comedians.

2. There are more women than men. Women have been the historical custodians of morals. But women have been emancipated, and American males are bewildered and confused by the aggressive, permissive, inviting behavior of girls and women.

Bronfenbrenner[4] after examination of the data cited by Bronson, Katten, and Livson (1959) pointed to a shift over the recent years in the "pattern of role differentiation within the family." He says:

In succeeding generations the relative position of the father *vis à vis* the mother is shifting with the former becoming increasingly more affectionate and less authoritarian and the latter becoming more important as the agent of discipline, especially for boys.

---

4 Urie Bronfenbrenner, "The Changing American Child: A Speculative Analysis," *Journal of Social Issues*, Vol. 17, No. 1 (1961), 6–18. Reprinted in Seidman, *op. cit.*

If marriage, childbearing and the custody of that old-fashioned commodity—chastity—lie in woman's realm then the emancipation of women, the change in their status, their leaving the home to work, their ambition to find mates for daughters are factors in any assessment of the causes and the effects of changes in social patterns of behavior of the young.

3. The devil may not have made the city, but he did find refuge there. America is about 80 per cent urban. Rural eighteenth- and nineteenth-century America was not morally pure, but life in the city is not the life of the familial village. City life raises all the problems Conant, Greer, Mack, Chandler and others have reported.

4. Shaw once said that the invention of cheap, convenient contraceptive devices was the greatest invention of man. Those concerned about the population explosion would agree. The historic penalties for illicit sex have been disease and unwanted children. The elimination of these dangers has also eliminated many of the restraints on sex.

The fact that the very young in elementary and high school have no knowledge of or access to these devices is attested by the rise in venereal disease and illegitimacy, in this age group.

5. What was once secret is now common knowledge. Adolescent high school and college culture was once sealed off from adult life—but no more. Freud's emphasis on sex has been taken up by the magazine and movie industries. High school students are free to read such books and to see plays by Tennessee Williams—and they understand what they read and hear and see.

6. Among other causes which might be decisive are the following:

A. Adult behavior at cocktail parties which youngsters are allowed to observe.

B. The trend toward cocktail parties as the "smart" prelude to a senior ball.

C. The tyranny of the young in the evolving permissive doctrine of demand feeding—the abdication of parental control.

D. Unchaperoned dates and youth parties.

E. The junior year in Europe which brings students into a permissive university culture without preparing them to cope with it.

Keeping Social Activities Pure

In our rapidly changing culture, adults worry about the young much as have other adults in all periods of history—except, perhaps, that they worry more and give up sooner. What can educational authorities do about the social-sexual patterns of living being evolved by today's youth?

Answers range from the extreme permissiveness—"treat them as adults"—of the Ivy League colleges to the rigid supervision of the 1890 Mid-western Bible belt teachers' colleges. The solution lies in striking a balance between these extremes:

1. Students have rights as well as desires and ideals.
2. Schools and colleges have some part of the responsibility for the moral if not the spiritual welfare of the young.
3. Parents pay the bills and they, too, have rights and hopes and ideals.

Educational institutions must find a way to guide the young—and the adults—to social relations that are personally satisfying yet consonant with traditional ideals. These are not easily won goals, but to aspire to less is not in the American public school tradition.

School officials and college deans have tried many solutions. The catalogue of attempts to "protect" the young would be a long one. The approach has, of course, been to impose rules, regulations, and restrictions—not education that is realistic and relevant. A list of things tried includes:

1. Expulsion of all students and dismissal of all teachers who get married. (The military academies still apply this rule to students.)
2. Expulsion of students and dismissal of teachers who become pregnant.
3. Censorship of all books and magazines. (Most of the post-Freudian novels and plays and all sociopsychological and anthropological books on sex would be barred.)
4. Expulsion from dances and parties of all students who have had wine or cocktails or anything alcoholic to drink.
5. Elimination of all "social" activities in the elementary school.
6. Postponement of dancing clubs, dances, and all dancing instruction until Grade 10 or 11.
7. Surrender to parents all responsibility for social activities and

moral surveillance; reconstitution of schools and colleges as exclusively intellectual institutions.

8. Abandonment of coeducation.

9. Radical de-emphasis of social activities. Limitation of such activities to formal teas and receptions.

10. Distraction of students from social pursuits through a sound and challenging academic program.

11. Enlistment of the churches and parents in a cooperative effort to reinstitute square dances, box suppers, and other social activities of a less provocative nature.

12. Elimination of cost reductions on tickets for couples.

13. Prohibition of all "couple" affairs from the high school-approved programs.

14. Establishment of rules forbidding any student to leave the gym, dance floor, or other center of a social activity.

15. Elimination of intermissions at dances.

16. Prohibition of private transportation; insistence on exclusive use of school buses.

17. Provision of many chaperones and policemen, especially at the parking lot.

18. Establishment of "codes."

19. Expulsion of couples who go steady.

20. Expulsion of couples caught holding hands on the campus or in the halls.

21. Adoption of girls' uniform designed by the local ministerial association.

22. Elimination of motion pictures as school entertainment or instructional instruments.

23. Establishment of a curfew for all youth under eighteen (to be enforced by a special squad of policemen and policewomen).

24. Establishment of compulsory home and family-life courses (including sex education) beginning in the fifth grade and continuing through high school and college.

25. Emphasis on religion. Elimination of secular public education and establishment of church control of all education.

26. Surrender to the tide of changed patterns of social behavior.

27. Restriction of married high school students to attendance at classes only.

The point should be emphasized, as Russell and others have, that the moralistic approach is doomed to failure. The lesson of history is clear. It is equally clear that choices are made by individuals in terms of their own values and ideals guided by their intelligence. This suggests that the way the younger generation thinks, feels, and acts is a product of all the influences to which it is subject. These influences, in all their many forms, constitute education. Schools provide only a part of the education of the young. If it is agreed—and of course it isn't—that something must be done to raise the standards of social life of youth, the attack must be total. Different, better, higher, ideals and values must be implanted, cultivated and rewarded.

Changes will be needed all along the line, and in every corner of our culture. Everything—book publishing, movie production, parental social activities, newspaper editing, marriage laws, divorce laws, teacher education, school curriculums, and school life will need to be modified—and drastically. To name all the changes, even without any elaboration, would fill a big book.

No hope can be entertained that Americans will make the sweeping changes required.

Can nothing, then, be done? Have we to surrender to all the newer patterns of social life? Is there no hope that new in-migrants to our cities, the depressed of the slums, the favored in our suburbs, and the "good kids from good homes" can grow up to adulthood, adding to rather than repudiating our cherished American ideals? Can the number of divorces, remarriages, broken homes and unhappy homes be reduced, if not completely eliminated? Can well-meaning and devoted parents do nothing? Are the churches powerless? Are the schools impotent?

Any survey of the literature dealing with school and college social life will disclose little more than a restricted, moralistic surveillance as answer to this question. But philosophers, psychologists, and educators have made various suggestions which can be used as general guides to a widely cooperative program.

1. Trust human intelligence—even the intelligence of the young.
2. Have confidence in the inherent tendency of humans to seek the good, the better. (See Maslow, ASCD 1962 Yearbook and the Society for the Scientific Study of Altruism.)[5]
3. Be willing to accept the fact that the different is not automatically or necessarily bad.
4. Counter misinformation with scientific facts.

---

[5] A. L. Maslow, in *Personality Symposium*, W. Wolff (ed.), (New York: Grune and Stratton, 1950), pp. 11–34. See also his *Some Basic Propositions of a Growth and Self-Actualizing Psychology*, in the *1962 Yearbook of the Association for Supervision and Curriculum Development*, Chap. 4.

5. Start free communication between parent and child very early with the very young in the home.

6. Build systematized and sequential programs of instruction.

7. Never judge a person's value by a few actions; never label acts "wrong" or "stupid" without a thorough knowledge of all circumstantial factors.

CHAPTER VI

Athletics

Sports and games are muscular activities in varied combinations. These are vestiges of ancient survival techniques. Running, throwing, jumping, swimming, and striking were once used to get food and to meet danger. They are now combined into many forms which occupy a large part of the recreational life of persons fortunate enough to live in cultures which have time left to play after basic needs have been satisfied.

American schools were quite inevitably patterned after English models. Their athletic programs, therefore, stress games and sports rather than the massed calisthenics popular on the Continent. Even today, a large share of the required physical education is made up of games rather than of formal exercises. Even dancing may be included. The vigor of some dance forms suggests that the participants should be given gym credit.

Americans bowl, golf, sail, fish, and climb mountains by the millions, and spend billions in the process. A Yale graduate employed by a large firm asked: "How do you get noticed around here?" He was told: "One way is to go to our annual outing and hit a homerun in the softball game."

An American driving through continental Europe cannot help but be impressed by the difficulty of spotting schools and universities. The dominant feature of the town and countryside is the cathedral. The traveler will see more schools and more playing fields in the short run from Dover to London than in a thousand miles of driving through France. The American instruction in gymnasiums, baseball fields, playgrounds, tennis courts, parks, and sport palaces is testimony to our devotion to games and sports and to the wealth required to indulge that devotion.

On the American frontier a sport was made of barn-raising. Whenever time was available, the turkey-shoot, the husking bee, and the elimination of a marauding bear or bobcat was turned into a game. From shooting seed-eating crows to skeet-shooting, Americans have found life more pleasant through sport, and have made a sport of almost everything.

As early as 1930, according to Terry, 29 per cent of the student activities in 82 urban junior high schools were in athletics of some kind.[1] If Americans play to win, while the British play for fun (as the historian Commager maintained), it is in keeping with the traditions of each country. In debate, as in athletics, even junior high school and elementary school students want to win. American athletic programs are characterized by size, elaborate equipment, organization, and paying customers.

It is clear that sports and games, from major-league baseball to hopscotch, are important in American life and therefore in American educational life. The late President Kennedy introduced a new note when he linked sports to physical fitness and national strength. If education is a weapon and fit Americans are patriotic Americans, loyalty to country may replace the older motivation for inter-institutional contests and sandlot baseball.

The Soviet Union puts physical culture high on the priority list of youth training. On the opening day of the huge stadium, the Apartakiad, outside Moscow, "Fifteen hundred Moscow school children . . . were followed by 2,300 members of the Trudorye Sports Club. Then came 1,000 students from the State Central Institute of Physical Culture. Finally, 2,300 athletes participated in mass calisthenics. . . . Then began the great sports competition finals."[2]

American physical education and recreational programs range from the Saturday football game with thousands of paying spectators to a noon-hour ping-pong contest. In most states, physical education is mandated by law, but the problem of providing credit toward a diploma has not been resolved. Health is an avowed objective of education, but the honor students at graduation may be overweight, or seriously malnourished, or have fallen arches and a mouthful of cavities.

The dividing line between the credit curriculum and the extra-curriculum is unclear. The ability to swim, for example, is required in some institutions for graduation. The list of noncredit sports

---

[1] Paul W. Terry, *Supervising Extracurricular Activities in the American Secondary School* (New York: McGraw-Hill Book Company, 1930).

[2] *The New York Times,* October 14, 1956.

common in American schools and colleges includes activities from archery to yachting. Except as sports form a part of the required physical education program, the bulk of the athletic program is in the noncredit or extracurriculum. This lack of clarity is of more than academic interest, for the inclusion of such activities in the credit curriculum is a measure of their importance and a controlling factor in the management of programs whether in the physical or the ideational realm. Where credits are given for physical education, or health education, or recreation, the matter is generally of no great significance to faculties, students, or parents. Significantly, almost nobody fails required physical education courses. Although too many young American men cannot pass the physical examination administered to draftees by the military, the standards for graduation from high school and college have not been raised.

The American image of schooling has not progressed to the point where an honor student can be denied a diploma if he is not physically fit. The educational drive in the 1960's is for academic excellence, not health and vigor. Sewing, typing, driver education, and other life-adjustment elements of the American school were attacked in the drive for educational reform. Significantly, no one has called for the elimination of health education, physical education, and recreation. On the other hand, few have campaigned for the imposition of higher standards in these areas.

School sports are in the British and American educational tradition and that tradition has a long history. It is clear, however, that the school is still dominantly an academic institution. The college-preparatory function of the secondary school has persisted and, to a large extent, is the measure of quality in education.

Athletics are fun and perhaps that is the way it should be. To move fun activities into the credit curriculum might entail losses a bedeviled world ought not to be made to endure.

France, under de Gaulle, has instituted a program for physical strength as part of the famous baccalaureate examinations. A Lycée boy student, for example, had to be able to run sixty meters in eight seconds or less. Weekly busloads of boys and girls were transported to the municipal stadium at Aix-en-Provence to take their tests. In the European tradition, of course, the emphasis was on the final examination rather than on the improvement of performance throughout the term. Also, the centralization of control in the national capital is a policy Americans are reluctant to adopt.

Education is reserved to the states, and large pieces of authority are reserved by local boards of control.

But the main problem is that Americans are not yet ready to take health and physical vigor seriously. If cigarette sales could rise after the publication of all the medical evidence accumulated in the 1950's and 1960's, we certainly are not ready to impose high standards of health as a requirement for graduation from high school and college.

Sports and athletic games are now and will (in the foreseeable future, at least) remain in the nonrequired, noncredit curriculum. The total program in athletics and sports may be classified in large headings as follows:

1. *Required physical education:* credit or noncredit; generally mandated by law.

2. *Electives in the noncredit activity program.* There is much duplication between the required and the extracurriculum. Soccer, for example, is taught in required physical education classes and is also engaged in as an extracurricular activity. There is also a great deal of election in the required physical education work. Sometimes walking may fulfill the physical education requirement for a student who has chosen a mountain-climbing course.

3. *Competitive organized athletics:*
   A. Intramural
   B. Interinstitutional

4. *Unorganized, noncompetitive, recreational athletics and sports.* The carryover values of such activities are high. Hiking, golf, tennis, boating, skiing, and many noon-hour activities would be included here.

5. *Remedial services:* for correction of bad posture, fallen arches, lack of coordination.

6. *Associated activities:* e.g., those of the cheer leaders, the band, the majorettes; half-time events (from crowning queens to close-order drill marching); trampoline exhibits; sport nights; play days; pep assemblies; award dinners; fathers' clubs; officiating clubs; carnivals.

Objectives

Athletics developed as a student activity. The students had no thought of objectives, aims, or purposes. Athletics simply satisfied the need of students—especially boys—to be active; they constituted a release from the forced inactivity of the classroom and chapel.[3]

Later, the school authorities took over the management of sports and games, and established a systematized program of physical education. The basic class work consisted largely of German-type exercises, but these soon gave way to games, sports, and even dancing. State laws were passed mandating physical education for all students in public schools. Physical education was required in most colleges in the freshman and sophomore years.

Objectives were formally stated by the new specialists in the new programs of health, physical education, and recreation. Almost every human value can—and has—been suggested as an aim of athletic activities. Among these will be found physical and organic growth, social traits, good citizenship, sound moral ideals, emotional stability, safety skills, recreation, verbal learning, self-discipline, and health.

In 1954, the Educational Policy Commission concluded: "We believe in athletics as an important part of the school physical education program. We believe that the experience of playing athletic games should be part of the education of all children and youth who attend school in the United States."[4]

That active sports and games are beneficial to participants is accepted by all, even by those who do not participate. A proviso, however, must be added: the values accrue only when the participant's attitudes and motives are pure and when regard is taken of the limits of his endurance. Spectator sports and complex team games, on the other hand, have little carryover value into adult life.

Social scientists see in American athletics a special set of values not ordinarily discussed in the literature on health, physical education, and recreation. These should be briefly noted.

1. There is a vocational value. Baseball, hockey, basketball, and football are big business outside the ivy-covered walls. The skillful player on a college team may become a professional and make money—a lot of money. Later, he might become an announcer, a sportswriter, an endorser of razors and breakfast foods, or a sales-

---

[3] See Frederick Rudolph, *The American College and University* (New York: Alfred A. Knopf, Inc., 1962).

[4] Eductional Policies Commission, *School Athletics: Problems and Policies* (National Education Association, 1954), p. 3.

man of sports equipment. Americans generally accept the value of scholastic athletics, though some reformers do not. If Lujack made more money than the president of Notre Dame, the fault, if any, lies with American values—not with the school and college athletics. (Of course, there are those who regret the encroachment of vocationalism in any form.)

2. School and college athletics stimulate research and inventiveness in nutrition, equipment, and physiology. The merits of isometric and isotonic contraction are under intensive study. The fiberglass pole raised the height of the pole-vault record. Special equipment, new materials, and a host of other products were stimulated by athletics. The whirlpool baths used for sprains and muscular disorders developed for athletes no doubt were helpful to those who promoted rehabilitation programs after World War II.

3. Athletics offered many opportunities for scientists engaged in high acceleration studies. The Popular Science Magazine reported:[4]

. . . Dr. Stephen E. Reid of Northwestern University's medical school . . . installed miniature acceleration-measuring devices in the helmets of two Northwestern fullbacks, connected to radio transmitters in their shoulder pads. The study is aimed at developing safer football helmets.

4. Team loyalty provides the sense of identification—of belonging—so much needed in an age of impersonalization and alienation. If the citizen is concerned about the successes and failures of his alma mater's football team, or of the Yankees or Dodgers, something good happens. He may find only a class or status symbol, but he may also derive a sense of attachment, of loyalty, of purpose.

America is a united nation, in part at least, because of athletics. When President Eisenhower called for "team spirit," all Americans knew what he meant. To have "two strikes" on a person, to "strike out," to "win in a walk," to "play the game," to "make a comeback"—these expressions are part of our American language. Ask any person who was King of Swat, and if he doesn't say, "Babe Ruth," you will know he is not an American.

Athletics serve America and some Americans by providing an escape—from poverty, rejection, and alien status. George Washington Carver is less well known than Joe Louis or Jackie Robinson.

---

[4] *Popular Science Magazine*, Vol. 184, No. 1 (January 1964).

It may well be that a nation that plays together stays together. It is more than an accident that integration in athletics preceded integration in the classroom.

In athletics, most moral issues are brought out into the open and fought out in the public view. Cheating, bribery, athletic "scholarships," and amateur standing are moral issues at the level both of the man in the street and the college president. The hard slide and the hard tackle are legal and proper. Clipping and roughing the kicker and high sticking are punishable and for very good reasons. "Right" and "wrong" are not vague concepts on the playing field; they are active principles bred into each new generation through games and sports. It was not only an interest in athletics which led a new free nation of Africa to arrange for some of its young men to come to America to learn our athletic ways.

Dangers and Problems

With athletics, as with any good thing, the potential for evil exists. From deep-dish apple pie to atomic power, the good use or the bad is determined by people. Honest and intelligent persons can and do disagree as to what is good and what is evil. The following is a brief catalogue of some of the issues and the problems in athletics as they have developed in American education.

Competition is a fact of life, and after Darwin, a part of evolution. Cooperation is also a fact of life, but it stops in large part at the scrimmage line and at the frontiers of the nation. That athletics and poker are competitive is no small part of their appeal. To play to win is not in itself a mortal sin. America's military academies make much of competitive athletics. Cheating, however, is condemned. If competition within the rules is called *the pursuit of excellence,* a new face is put on competition. To win at all costs is to pervert the pursuit of excellence. To win by paying the coach more than the principal or president brings a moral issue out in the open. Rule books and officials take care of the game, but only the integrity of educators can eliminate undeserved athletic scholarships, neglect of intellectual values, exploitation of players for personal or institutional gain, and the many other seductive traps.

Balance, proper perspective, and an even keel are all desirable, but seldom thrilling. We are admonished not to put all our eggs in one basket, and so seek and hold to the *via media*. Athletics, or more accurately, interinstitutional, competitive athletics are subject to excessive demands on money, time, facilities, and attention. No issue in American education has been more hotly debated than the emphasis on stadium athletics. College teams, during the school term, tour the continent to play in its far corners on successive Saturdays. Whole towns shut down when the local high school is in the state championship playoffs, and nations celebrate when their Little League Team wins the big one across the border. Even in the Olympics, designed to promote international understanding, reporters keep an unofficial score to see how America and the Soviet Union are doing.

The issue, of course, is crystal clear. The human need for adventure and thrills gets in the way of the quiet satisfactions of intellectual work, the pleasures of a moonlight stroll, the joys of a "for-fun" interclass game of softball at a picnic. Even so intellectual a game as bridge has its national and international competitive phases. Any hope that human beings will soon have no need for massive distractions and be content with the quiet simple pleasures is a vain one.

When the manager of the Mets says to a rookie, "Turn in your suit. You are going to the minors," no one is morally offended or unhappy except the diehard fans of the deposed player. When the college coach says, "Turn in your suit and your convertible," there are sharp twinges of conscience in the academic world—and there should be. Schools and colleges are not, in America, single-purpose institutions; they are both intellectual and social institutions. They are a test slice of life—as broad and as demanding as life itself. The intellectual concern should be the dominant one, whether it be directed to the study of symbolic logic, business administration, education, or cement under stress.

The fact that very few Oberlin, Reed, Swarthmore, or Amherst men become professional football players may not be a tribute to the virtue of de-emphasis or an achieved balance; nor is it a sign of lack of ability. It is an indication of something else. That "something else" could be wider economic opportunities, job contacts, or the fact that a place in the economy has been provided elsewhere. Individuals, institutions, minority groups, and nations that have attained status no longer need athletics as a way to self-confidence, to recognition, or to power. They can afford to de-emphasize the importance of sports.

The Saturday afternoon athletic spectacle attracts larger crowds than any other entertainment. That educational institutions should provide entertainment for the academic community and for the public is highly debatable. A lecture on art forms or on the reading problems of left-handed children are informative and constructive, but rarely entertaining. The question is not whether amusement is desirable, but whether it is the proper function of deliberate education.

The related problems of financing athletics, gambling, extensive travel, extended seasons, and television complicate the issue. It is true that if the schools and colleges do not give the public what it wants and do not provide the capable player with an opportunity to display his ability and interest, some other agency will. In an absurd world, distracting entertainment is as necessary as tranquilizers. The fact that, historically, the universities of Europe did not engage in such activities is completely irrelevant; what is relevant is that American educational institutions do. The Institute For Advanced Study and the Princeton Tiger can coexist in a small college town, as can the Rockefeller Institute and the New York Yankees in New York.

And why not, provided only that the common ethical commitments are honored? Whether the Boys Club of America or the schools give the poor boys of the city recreation is a problem of economy and efficiency, not one of ethics or philosophy.

Why any college team should play in Madison Square Garden and why championship playoffs and tournaments and postseason bowl games should be held are questions to be answered by Americans in terms of their values. And such values are catholic and pluralistic in America. Why should a college glee club go on the road to amuse alumni and raise money? The difference between big leg muscles and small throat muscles is one of degree, not of kind. There is much more to life than that which resides above the ears and is visible above the desk top. It should always be remembered that America made the school—not the church or (in our era) the home—the focus of corporate life.

Gate receipts keep schools and colleges in business. Every small college can go into a deep financial hole with an advance out of operation funds of $100,000 for interinstitutional competition. Boards of education, of trustees, or of overseers are neither willing nor able to make admission to all athletic events free. If spectators were barred, alumni would go elsewhere to spend their money. If admission were made free, athletics would be as starved as the departments of ancient languages. If quality were to be maintained without gate receipts, the public would have to pay through general taxes.

American schools and colleges are caught in a financial trap. Their freedom lies, perhaps, in two things. First, they must be honest, ethical, and fair. If schools are in the amusement business—as indeed they are—they must represent the best ethical standards. Secondly, they must remember that there is more to life than health, physical powers, and recreation. Intelligence is really man's only weapon in his struggle for survival.

CHAPTER VII

Fraternities and Sororities

A Doubtful Activity

Secret social organizations—whatever they may be in colleges—are not technically high school student activities, because they do not have the approval and supervision of the faculty and administration. By definition, such approval is necessary to qualify an activity as a part of the third curriculum. In the strict academic sense, this discussion should not appear in a book on student activities in American education, for secret societies are considered by many to fall into the same category as dope rings, underworld mobs, and street gangs. In actual fact, however, sororities and fraternities are very much a part of the life of many high schools and most colleges. The literature, both general and professional, is crowded with discussions of high school fraternities and sororities. As early as 1834 many college presidents questioned the merits of college fraternities. Such societies were attacked as being anti-religious, antidemocratic, antivirtue, and anti-intellectual. Few phases of the noncredit life of American education have received more general attention or been of more concern to the authorities in and out of academic halls.

The Secret Society Problem Is Current

Roberts and Draper[1] stated in 1928 that:

High school fraternities and sororities reached their climax as vital educational issues twenty to thirty years ago, remained sharp and mixing problems up to 1920 and have been slowly losing ground during the last ten years. . . . Their last refuge appears to be the private boarding schools of secondary rank, whence they spread out to include the more or less colorless social groups in the public high schools.

[1] A. C. Roberts and E. M. Draper, *Extraclass and Intramural Activities in High Schools* (Boston: D. C. Heath & Company, 1928), p. 149.

Roberts and Draper were too optimistic: the fraternity problem has not yet been solved. The National Education Association and The National Association of Secondary School Principals are still concerned over this problem. As late as 1961,[2] the Tulsa, Oklahoma, public schools had a page on fraternities in their bulletin to parents. Many communities are bothered by all the problems of secret, extralegal, self-perpetuating clubs and societies. The form may be new —as for example, the leather-jacketed hotrodders, the cheerleaders, the drinking gangs, the cellar mobs, the shoplifters—but the problems are much the same. College students of the early and middle nineteenth century rebelled against the sterile classical curriculum, the impersonal and chilly dormitories, and the dreary routine of prayers and sermons to find joy and warmth and close friendships in their fraternities. Millions of present-day adolescents are rebelling against something which causes them to form their own gangs. We always, it seems, have a youth problem.

It is clear that the "youth problem" is never solved, for in a dynamic society each younger generation must grow up in a new environment. No two generations tread the same path. The concern of the school authorities over the student-initiated societies was expressed in the National Education Association proceedings as early as 1904 and continues to be expressed now.[3]

A new serious look at fraternities in colleges was being taken in the late 1950's and 1960's. Maturing America may be outgrowing fancy costumes and secret rituals. In the colleges, religious and racial lines are being banished. Help week is replacing hell week. Yale Daily News and the university radio, in 1954, refused to publicize the names of men tapped for Skull and Bones, Book and Snake, and the other secret societies. The free air of a working democracy and a democracy at work may eventually make obsolete the mask, the hood, the sheet, the secret password, and even the burning cross.[4]

In a very real sense, the problem of secret, self-perpetuating, social fraternities is the fault of teachers and administrators. Although it is fruitless to blame the college faculties of the early

---

[2] *Your Child and Your School*, Tulsa Public Schools, Tulsa, Oklahoma.

[3] See *Proceedings of the National Education Association* and the *Bulletin of the National Association of Secondary School Principals*.

[4] See, for example, David Boroff, *Showdown on Fraternity Row, The New York Times Magazine*, November 11, 1962.

1800's and the secondary school teachers of the early 1900's, it is worthwhile noting that youth will be served one way or another. If the school, the church, or the community cannot meet the fundamental needs of youth, then youth will find its own way. Had the high schools changed the pattern of school life and work rapidly enough, secret societies might never have become the stubborn growth which still has not been cut out of the school life.

A Difference Makes a Difference

Youth groups of all kinds exist in schools, churches, neighborhoods and communities. Some or all of these organized groups may be officially sponsored by the school. They are not fraternities and should not be condemned as such, because they are neither secret nor are new members selected by the present members independent of any outside agency.

The basketball squad is a group of carefully selected students, and frequently develops into a friendship group. What makes it different from a fraternity is that any student may try out for the team. The skills necessary for membership are understood by all; the judgment is made openly; the captain and the coaches make the choices and take the responsibility. These differences in standards and operation are crucial. Legislative enactments and rulings by boards or faculty would be more effective if more care was exercised in defining the features of organizations against which the laws or the rulings were directed.

No school organization needs to take everybody who wants to join.[5] Special qualifications for membership in different organizations can and should be set up. Even the members of the student council, the chief agency of democratic student participation in school management, are selected in terms of special qualifications for leadership, service, and management. In the same way, the traffic squad, the photography club, and the German club may have distinctive and restrictive membership requirements. The differences between such clubs and the secret societies are made clear

---

[5] Democracy is, of course, a concept of very high interpretative level. A restaurant can set prices so high that most Americans could not afford to enter to have dinner. Why, then, could it not close its doors to women, to redheads, or to other groups? It is clear the fraternity-equality problem is complex.

by the fact that the school principal can freely and openly attend and participate in the work of the former, but not of the latter.

History

The first college fraternity of which there is record appeared at the College of William and Mary in 1750. It adopted the name "The Flat-Top Club." It was secret, literary, and social in character. It held regular meetings, had a special handshake, and a badge.

There is a belief that Phi Beta Kappa might have arisen from this fraternity. Phi Beta Kappa was founded in 1776, also at the College of William and Mary. It was the first society to adopt a Greek name. Its activities were similar to those of the literary societies of the day; they included debates and discussions of current issues.

A number of college social fraternities appeared during the early 1800's, displaying many of the characteristics of the earliest ones. Formal ceremonies marked the admission process; they included all the trappings held dear by college fraternities until very recent times. It is interesting to note that at Union College, where the first "modern" fraternity was established, a conference was held on the fraternity problem in 1963. One participant called fraternity rituals "badly dated Mickey Mouse stuff."

The first sorority, Alpha Delta Pi, was founded in 1851 at Wesleyan College, Macon, Georgia; and the second was started the following year at the same college. Both remained strictly local for many years before they took Greek names and were ready for expansion. These early sororities were modeled after the fraternities.

Probably the first high school fraternity was Omega Tau, founded in Council Bluffs, Iowa in 1859.[6] The parent chapter of this fraternity was inactive at various intervals between 1861 and 1893, when it was revived by two of the original founders. In point of continuous operation, Alpha Zeta, founded in Schenectady, New York, in 1869, may be called the oldest fraternity in secondary

---

[6] There is no definitive history of high school secret societies. H. C. McKown states in his *Extracurricular Activities* (New York: The Macmillan Company, 1952), p. 175. "That the first high school fraternity is supposed to have been started in 1876." See the *Encylopedia Americana* for a brief history of college Greek-letter societies and fraternities.

schools.[7] Theta Sigma, founded in Albany, New York, in 1887, is the oldest high school sorority.

The influence of these fraternities and sororities was not felt in the secondary schools until the beginning of the twentieth century when they began competing for honors in the school. It was at this time that secondary education in America began to accept the multitudes and to add other goals to the college-preparatory function.

Plan of Organization

There are many different types of secret societies in the different high schools throughout the country. A society may be either national or local; that is, it may be nationwide, or it may be restricted to only one school. There are some that are organized with faculty approval, and there are those which are organized without such approval. Some have limited membership; others admit anyone who wishes to join. Some are organized with parental approval. Some adopt Greek names; others use English letters or words as a name. They all have in common passwords, mottoes, insignia, songs, regular meetings, special initiation activities, and a self-perpetuating character.

The national fraternal society is often more complex and better organized than the group which is strictly local. Most of the formal secret societies have honorary members who act as advisors. These are faculty members, alumni, or other adults in the community. Members in the secret societies in high schools may be drawn from all four grade levels, or only from the upper two or three, depending on the school and the size of the organization. (Junior high schools appear to have escaped the secret society problem.) The officers of the society usually consist of the president, a vice-president, a secretary, a treasurer, and a marshal who may be concerned with finding new members and directing hell week (or help week) and the initiation activities. The meetings are held in school, if the group has the approval of the school; if it does not, meetings are

---

[7] *Shucis,* the newspaper of Schenectady High School (now Linton) reported in 1911 the celebration of the forty-first anniversary of Alpha Zeta. In the same year, *Shucis* described the work of the Interfraternity Council and its rules and regulations.

usually held at the members' homes. Few high school secret societies have their own clubhouse.

The fraternity or sorority holds many parties and dances throughout the year. In some instances, these events are for members only; in other cases, they are open to the whole school and advertised openly in the school. These affairs are designed to raise money for the society.

Secret societies differ greatly, depending on their location and the general social climate. In one place, they may be as formal as the college fraternity or sorority. In other places, they may be only a group of students who stick together, wear identical sweaters, and call themselves a fraternity or sorority. Of special importance is the fact that any group, such as the National Honor Society, the cheerleaders, or the Hi-Y may take on some of the undesirable characteristics of a secret society if current members pick the new members year after year and thus become, in effect, self-perpetuating.

Why Secret Societies Persist

The fact that secret societies are and will be a problem for a long time cannot be too strongly emphasized. The problem has and will persist for very definite reasons, many of which have their roots deep in human nature, especially in adolescent human nature.

1. All individuals crave security, and the chief source of security is companionship. Loneliness is, for most humans, the chief horror of life. Misery loves company, and joy and adventure must be shared to be fully enjoyed. Young adolescents are especially in need of security, for they are just beginning to make their own new way in a complex world. For most of their early lives, the home has satisfied all their needs. When they reach the high school age, the home—especially the modern home—is no longer enough. The secret society provides a feeling of closeness and brotherhood or sisterhood. In many cases the members swear oaths to be friends, helpers, and to stand by one another. In the fraternity or sorority, young people find companions on whom they can depend. The emblem, the pin, the jacket proclaim to the world that the individual does not stand alone, but that he will be supported and defended by his group in all his enterprises.

2. Closely knit secret societies are a convenience to youth. They make partners for dating, parties, hunting, skiing, and fishing easy to find. The young person who is a member of a fraternity has someone to go to the movies with. Such societies personalize human relationships.

3. Fraternities and sororities give status to the individual. Membership proclaims to the world that the individual was sought out and selected by his peers to be a brother or a sister. The tragedy of rejection is avoided. The mantle of status may also have financial and cultural aspects; but the mere fact of having been chosen to be part of a select group is enough to make membership desirable. The nonmember is wont to hasten to explain that his college did not have fraternities, or that he was asked to join but could not afford to or did not choose to. In August 1963, Phiota of Phi Delta Theta[8] reported that 70 per cent of the United States Senators and 40 per cent of the Representatives in the 88th Congress were members of college fraternities.

4. Such societies confer school-related benefits on their members. Members are encouraged by their fellows to try out for teams and to become candidates for office. They are assured that their fellows will help them in all possible ways—and sometimes more than they should.

When these facts are considered, it is little wonder that all efforts of school faculties and state legislatures have not eliminated secret societies from school and collegiate life. These efforts have not succeeded, not only for the basic reasons listed above, but for the following practical reasons.

1. The school has not been able to satisfy the basic cravings of its students.

2. Parents enjoy the status and prestige of their own college fraternity life and the reflected status of their children's having "made a good fraternity."

3. Teachers and parents are not all convinced that the evils of such societies outweigh their benefits.

4. Adults are ignorant of or blind themselves to the evils in the local situation. They say, "It cannot happen here."

5. There is a real legal question of the rights of the individual to choose his own friends and to assemble with them.

---

[8] Phi Delta Theta, Ohio Iota Chapter, Denison University, Granville, Ohio, 1963.

6. The never-ending search for a balance between equality and individual freedom has meaning in daily life as well as in the classroom.

7. In an ever-changing world, values, mores, and needs change. Thus the adult world and the world of the young inevitably differ from one another.

Charges Against Fraternities

The list of charges against secret social groups in high school and college is long. Some are, of course, superficial; but others go to the heart of our democratic ideals. Among the charges may be listed the following.

1) They are undemocratic:
   a. They are secret.
   b. They are self-perpetuating bodies.
   c. They practice segregation and separatism.
   d. They foster divisive loyalties and false standards of value.
2) They are anti-intellectual:
   a. They depreciate scholarship.
   b. They interfere with studies.
3) They obstruct the student life in other activities:
   a. They practice petty politics.
   b. They introduce low motives into elections and team play.
   c. They are detrimental to school spirit.

Perhaps the most frequent criticism, at least in popular magazines, is leveled against the abuses that occur during initiations. Examples of such abuse are too revolting to list. More fundamental objections are that they promote division of loyalty; that they are self-perpetuating; that they are exclusive and undemocratic; that they are clannish; that they do not promote scholarship and are, in fact, anti-intellectual; that they are divisive; and they are not under the control of the adult institutional authorities, of parents, or of alumni.

The most serious objection would appear to be that they are undemocratic. It is argued that no educational institution in a democracy has a right to exist if it bases membership on any qualification other than publicly known merit.[9]

---

[9] The fraternity debate in the 1950–60's was a part of the worldwide reappraisal of white-colored relationships from Cape Town to Williamsburg. Interestingly, religious segregation in Protestant, Catholic, and Jewish schools and fraternities, legion posts, and cemeteries was not of wide concern.

Countless stories are told of discrimination against students because of the kind of home their parents live in, the clothes they
wear, the drinking practices they adopt, the sexual standards they
adhere to, and many other reasons. These bases of selection are not
funny to the boy or girl who is rejected because of them.

The University of Michigan Survey Research Center reported
in 1962 that more fraternity men than independent students had
parents with college education, were better dressed, and dated
frequently. These findings would seem to indicate that selectivity on
the basis of financial status was practiced.

More serious is the problem of racial and religious discrimination. The issue came to a head after the desegregation ruling of the
Supreme Court in 1954, but it had been developing some years
before. In 1961 *Time* reported that twenty-two out of thirty-four
fraternities at the University of Michigan had bias clauses. At Stan-
ford University, Alpha Tau Omega pledged four Jewish boys in
violation of the national charter and was threatened with expulsion
from the national organization. Beta Theta Pi tapped a Negro student and was ordered by the national hierarchy to halt all initiations
"pending an investigation."

It has been argued that fraternities promote scholarship, but
Beverly Jean Smith, in *School Activities*,[10] and Sister Wendelin,
in *Clearing House*,[11] contradict this thesis. Sister Wendelin said:
"While I am not in a position to speak authoritatively of college
Greek-letter societies, I can say with conviction as a teacher in secondary schools, that 'eagerness in the pursuit of knowledge' is obviously not the binding link of high school fraternities and sororities."

The Michigan survey stated that nonfraternity men made better
grades than members. It was also reported that fraternity men tend
to choose business administration as a major field, while indepen-
dents tend to choose engineering, humanities, and the sciences.[12]

Greek-letter societies are hostile to the purposes of the school
in that they introduce an irrelevant element into other activities.
Time[13] mentioned an incident in which athletes refused to play with

---

[10] Beverly Jean Smith, *"I Belonged to a High School Sorority,"* School Activi-
tie* Vol. 21. No. 1 (September 1949), 5.

[11] Sister Wendelin, "Greek Letter Sore Spot," *Clearing House,* Vol. 20, No. 4
(December 1945), 201–204.

[12] *The Saturday Review,* December 15, 1962.

[13] "Gang Busters," *Time,* Vol. 53, No. 46 (January 17, 1949).

others who were not fraternity members. In view of this, and numerous similar incidents, it is well to ask whether it is just that some children should be deprived of school activities and organizations to which they are entitled. Milligan and Stover mentioned a similar incident described by a mother: "My daughter has always enjoyed athletics but has never gone out for any team because most of the members of the teams have been sorority girls who would refuse to throw the ball in her direction. The same thing happened in her regular gym periods again and again."[14]

Another occurrence reported by Milligan and Stover involved a scheduled hockey game that had been postponed a week. A girl who was a member of a sorority came to the coach to say that she could not play on the postponed date because it conflicted with a sorority social event. The coach, the high school principal, and a faculty committee considered the matter and decided that the game must be played. The game was played, but seventeen girls of a total of forty on the hockey team were absent. In this instance, it was obvious that loyalty to the sorority took precedence to loyalty to the school.

The Greek-letter societies frequently dominate the social and political life of the school. These organizations act as pressure groups, nominating and selecting candidates who owe allegiance to them. Thus secret societies become self-feeding organizations, growing more exclusive, more snobbish, and more divisive as they gain prestige.

There are many who think that members of a Greek-letter society gain polish and refinement. Sister Wendelin, in *Clearing House,* expresses a contrary opinion: "In my dealing with high school students, I have found that the argument that fraternity and sorority members are boys and girls of refinement carries little weight. Whenever I found such students to be conspicuous for their courtesy, and I admit I have in a number of cases, invariably they were boys and girls who acquired their manners at home."[15]

There is almost universal *official* agreement among school administrators, board of education members, state legislators, and the public that secret, self-perpetuating fraternities and sororities are

---

[14] J. P. Milligan and C. F. Stover, "High School Secret Societies: A National Problem," *American School Board Journal,* Vol. 115, No. 2 (August 1947), 26–28.

[15] Sister Wendelin, *op. cit.*

undesirable—if not actually a menace—at the high school level. Almost everything has been tried to eradicate them, from the expulsion of members from school to the levying of fines on administrators for failure to eliminate such societies. The fact, however, is that this *official* disapproval hides a widespread tacit approval. The fact must be faced that in many sections of the country parents are not convinced that high school fraternities and sororities are bad.

In Defense of Secret Societies

Stanch defenders of the college fraternity system are not hard to find, but educators who advocate the secret society system in the secondary schools are very rare indeed. Arguments for the defense of such societies are usually based on the constitutional guarantees of free assembly and the right of the individual to choose his own friends and to live his own life within the letter and spirit of the law. In general, the defenders emphasize the "reforms" that have been instituted.

Of the supporters of secondary school fraternities, Hulsey was perhaps the most articulate and convincing. He stated:

The public does not realize that every national high school fraternity supports scholarship, and all give an award of some type ranging from money for support of college education to medals and keys. It is also not commonly known that the commonly followed ritual of each organization is based upon the Holy Bible and by this ritual, each meeting is conducted and new members taken in.[16]

Hulsey claimed that national Greek-letter societies render service to the school and the community by performing acts of charity.

All national high school fraternities require their chapters to adopt needy families on Thanksgiving, Easter, and Christmas. . . . The National Association of High School Fraternities is a service organization ready to serve school and community.

As a spokesman for the Interfraternity Council of Secondary and Nonacademic Fraternities, Hulsey[17] charges the local and inde-

---

16 W. O. Hulsey, "Of the Fraternity," *School Activities*, Vol. 20, No. 1 (September 1948), 8–10. See also Gerald M. Van Pool, "Versus the High School Fraternity," *School Activities*, Vol. 21, No. 3 (November 1948), for a reply to Dr. Hulsey.

17 Hulsey, *op. cit.*, 9.

pendent fraternities with the abuses that are attributed to all Greek-letter societies. He further asserts that those fraternities which are associated with a national organization are well regulated and properly supervised.

In all national high school fraternities each chapter and every member works under the guidance of national officers, men of mature age and successfully established in their own private enterprises.

Perhaps the most frequent charge against fraternities is that they are flagrantly undemocratic and that they foster and promote senseless and revolting initiations. To these accusations Dr. Hulsey rejoins:

When the subject of fraternity is discussed, some imagine an exclusive, snobbish group delegated to hazing and obscenity. But this is not true, for as have all organizations, the national high school fraternity has "grown up" under proper guidance, tutoring, and careful direction of its alumni and national officers.

The charge of exclusiveness is answered by the statement that we cannot deny any "individual the prerogative of selecting his own friend."

On the positive side it is claimed that the reason for establishing a high school fraternity is to give young persons training in parliamentary procedure, correspondence, business relationships, and experience in working with fellow students.

The existence of fraternities in the high schools is indicative of the fact that they are serving some imperative need of the adolescents. Lawrence E. Vredevoe has suggested that they give young adults a chance to identify themselves with a small closed group which supplies:

1. Prestige (through restricted membership);
2. Secrecy (through closed meetings, initiation, special handshakes);
3. Identification with a group (through pins, insignia, sweaters, group activities);
4. Social recognition (through parties and other social affairs);
5. Allegiance (through support given individual members for school offices, help on athletic teams);
6. Adventure, fun, and so on (through initiations and other activities).[18]

---

[18] *Bulletin of the National Association of Secondary School Principals,* Vol. 32, No. 153 (March 1948).

On the College Front

Professor Crocker, faculty advisor to Sigma Alpha Epsilon, was reported in the Denison, Granville, Ohio *Alumni Bulletin* of May 1960 to have said to the students: "Why has Denison gone all out for the fraternity? At Denison you are more than a mind. . . . What residential houses are to Yale, the fraternities are to Denison." Professor Crocker went on to say that the intramural program is built on fraternity units, that fraternities were proud of their Phi Beta Kappas, Fulbright scholars, and Woodrow Wilson Fellows; that they fostered lasting friendships and loyalty to the alma mater.

Corrective Proposals

School officials and teachers must take some action on this problem. Concern for the welfare of youth cannot stop with the closing bell or at the edge of the school campus. The only defensible position is that secret societies composed of high school youth are potentially, if not currently, antithetical to the American dream. The approach adopted may be educative, regulatory, or legalistic. The following are the major procedures open to school authorities:

1. *Do nothing.* There may be no cause for concern. No organization of secret societies may exist in a particular school. The problem may have already been solved, or may never have arisen. Such an ideal situation may, in fact, exist; but the chances are good that the academic head is buried in the sand. The ritual of handwashing is open to school authorities, but those who avail themselves of this comfortable position are hard to find.

2. *Do nothing directly but everything positively.* The school faculty and interested parents may choose to make a flanking attack on secret societies. This consists in not condemning such societies except by inference. In a sense, this mode of handling the problem is the soft, safe, educator's method. It avoids open warfare. Nobody gets mad at anybody.

The specifics depend on the educational vision, ingenuity, and devotion of the staff to the cause. The fact that the process is slow must be accepted. Also, it is necessary that staff time, school facilities, and some money be available; for the high school staff selecting this approach must compete for the time and attention of youth against (in some cases) national organizations. The magnitude of the problem is clear when it is recalled that large private colleges with comparatively unlimited resources for house plans, house athletic programs, house buildings with generous if not luxurious facilities have not succeeded in twenty-five years in entirely eliminating secret fraternities. The Harkness-financed Harvard system was and is a positive endorsement of the "collegiate way," but the smaller nonofficial social units still survive.

This method requires that the school provide social, athletic, and recreational activities more attractive and more satisfying to youth than those the secret society can provide. It means that personal attention must be available on the highest possible level for security and prestige, for these will be sought by youth in one way or another. The persistence and the magnitude of the school dropout problem suggests the difficulty of meeting the needs of all American youth.

All the possible maneuvers cannot be recorded, but an illustration may make the approach clearer. Suppose a strong ranking fraternity has scheduled a fund-raising dance at the local country club or hotel during the Christmas vacation. The school could counter with a Christmas alumni dance, but the school dance must be "smoother" and "keener" than the fraternity party. The band must be better known, the vocalist a recording star, the refreshments more inviting. Prominent alumni of the school should be invited early and committed to the school affair in a definite and publicized way.

3. *Adopt and apply "sanitary" codes.* Those who want to retain secret social societies and those who see no hope of eliminating them may want to "clean them up." This same approach has been tried with intercollegiate athletics with some, if not yet complete, success. An attempt to deal with fraternities by establishing a code of conduct may smack of appeasement—a horrible word in the mind of the purists or the wholly committed.

In his article in *School Activities,* Hulsey[19] suggests that a code of ethics be adopted to insure that there will be no abuses in fraternities. This code provides:

1. Every school shall establish yearly scholastic awards.
2. Physical hazing and "foolish public initiations and demonstrations" shall be abolished.

---

[19] Hulsey, *op. cit.,* 9.

3. Pledging should be made purposeful and should emphasize sincerity, ability, and interest of each candidate.

4. The pledge period should be an informative one in which all candidates are instructed in the workings of the fraternities.

5. Drinking or gambling shall not be allowed at fraternity functions.

6. Close supervision should be given chapters by their governing bodies and alumni.

7. There should be a faculty sponsor.

4. *Enact punitive regulations.* School officials who want to make a frontal attack on the secret societies may attempt "to put them in their proper place" by board of education and faculty regulations. Such regulations are restrictive and punitive. The authority and power of school authorities is summoned against student members and their condoning and supporting parents. Regulations mean a fight or many fights. The school authorities' ultimate weapon is, of course, expulsion. The effectiveness of this way of handling the problem depends entirely on the support the school has among the people of the community and among the student body.

Some typical regulative enactments include the rules that:

1. No insignia other than official school insignia may be worn in the school on the campus, or at school functions.

2. No unauthorized organization may advertise or promote any function, activity, or social event on school bulletin boards, the school paper, or in any other way.

3. No unapproved organization, 50 per cent of whose membership is made up of students enrolled in the high school, may use the school facilities at any time for any purpose.

4. Any person who is a member of any organization not on the approved school list shall be ineligible for a position on any school team, either intermural or intramural, nor shall such persons be eligible for any office in any school organization.

5. *Resort to law.*[20] "There ought to be a law" is an admonition which has been heeded by those who would eliminate secret social societies from the life and work of the American high school. No aspect of American education outside general control and support has been the object of so much legislation.

Many state legislatures and local school boards have legally

---

[20] See Milligan and Stover, *op. cit.,* for a tabular summary of legal provisions by states. See also L. R. Kilzer, H. H. Stephenson, and H. O. Nordberg, *Allied Activities in the Secondary School* (New York: Harper & Row, Publishers, 1956), p. 108.

prohibited student membership in high school secret societies. Exclusion from participation in the extracurricular activities of the school, denial of credit for school work, denial of a diploma, and often suspension or expulsion from school are common penalties for violation of the state law or local school board rulings.[21]

The state statutes and school board rulings have been challenged on grounds that they are in excess of the school boards' authority; that they invade parental authority; that they are cruel and unusual punishment; that they are arbitrary, discriminatory, and unreasonable; that they deprive members of their liberty, property, and happiness without due process of law; that they violate natural rights; that they are a denial of equal protection of laws and an impairment of vested rights; that they constitute unwarranted paternalism; and that they could interfere with religious liberty.

A number of state courts have upheld prohibitory statutes against these contentions. The majority opinion holds that an:

. . . educational institution provided by the state is not a natural right but a public benefaction and those who seek to become beneficiaries of them must submit to such regulations and conditions as the law imposes as a prerequisite to participate.[22]

The point is also made that none of our liberties is absolute; all may be limited when required by common good or common decency. Only the Missouri State Court did not uphold the rulings against high school secret societies, stating that such rulings and penalties are "unjust, discriminate, and unsupported by right or reason."[23]

In Chicago, the school board went so far as to enact a rule that any principal who failed to abolish fraternities in his school would be discharged. In Ohio, a fine of ten to twenty-five dollars is the penalty for organizing or joining any secret society made up of pupils. The board of education is directed to investigate the existence of secret societies upon receipt of complaints, and to give formal cease and desist notice to any person found to be engaging in such activities in the public school. If this notice to stop is not obeyed, the superintendent or principal in charge is to suspend such pupil until he has complied with the order of the board.

---

[21] William R. Hood, *State Laws, School Regulations, and Judicial Decisions* (Washington, D.C.: City School Leaflet No. 7, 1923).

[22] See also Kitzer, *et al., op. cit.,* Chap. V.

[23] Daniel R. Hodgdon, "Fraternities in High School" *Clearing House,* Vol. 22, No. 2 (October 1947), 117–18.

The New York State Education Department stated its position in a letter to school administrative heads:

While there is no specific statute prohibiting fraternities, sororities, and secret societies in the public schools of this state, local school autorities have control over organizations of pupils which are in public schools. However, local school authorities have no jurisdiction over the private affairs of students who do not hold themselves representing the school or who do not meet on school property.[24]

In the School Law Review of *Clearing House,* Hodgdon states:

A pupil has the right to attend school and claim the benefits of the public school system only when he is willing to abide by the lawful rules prescribed for the conduct of the school by the board of education. . . .
A board of education may adopt rules in good faith if they are not clearly contrary and unreasonable. . . .
The board expressed the feeling that it cannot feel it has been true to its responsibilities unless it endeavors to guard in every way against false conceptions of superiority and the setting up of social distinctions.
Coggins, *et al., vs.* Board of Education of City of Durham 28 S.E. (2d) January 12, 1944.[25]

The legal difficulties of eliminating secret societies is illustrated by the fact that they were still a problem in Evanston[26] in 1958 despite a 1921 school law that held:[27]

Public school fraternity, sorority, or secret society is declared an organization inimical to the public good. Duty of public school boards to suspend or expel from school any pupil who shall be or remain a member of such fraternity, sorority, or society, or promise to join the same or solicit other persons to join the same. Unlawful for any person not enrolled in the public schools to solicit any public school pupil to join or pledge himself to join any such fraternity, sorority, or society or to attend a meeting thereof or any meeting where such organization is encouraged.

In 1945, the law was amended to provide suspension for viola-

---

[24] University of the State of New York, State Department of Education, February 25, 1946.
[25] Daniel R. Hodgdon, "Fraternities in High School," *Clearing House,* Vol. 22, No. 2 (October 1947), 117–18.
[26] *Here's Your High School,* Evanston Township High School, Evanston, Ill., April, 1958.
[27] Hood, *op. cit.*

tion and a fine of not less that twenty-five dollars nor more than one hundred dollars.[28]

The question naturally arises whether an approach combining any two or more of the six methods in sequence or concurrently might not prove most effective. The first, of course, if adopted makes all the others unnecessary. To combine the second and third might well arouse resistance and thus make the way of competition ineffective. The third and fourth might be used at the same time. The fifth and sixth are resorts to force and authority. The fifth might be a stage with six invoked only when denial of activity participation fails. Other combinations are possible. Competition —that is, making school life more attractive than fraternity life— and education might be used with the others. In the long run, only good schools and a populace convinced of the undesirability of secret societies will work.

---

[28] Illinois School Code, Article 31, p. 223, 1945.

CHAPTER VIII

A Look Ahead

From the founding of Harvard in 1636 and the Boston Latin School in 1635, Latin and Greek dominated the curriculum, entrance requirements, graduation standards, and commencement ceremonies of secondary and higher education. Even today Harvard commencements feature an essay in Latin read by a student —but this ceremony marks only a sentimental link with the past. The 1828 Yale report was a defense of the classical tradition which persisted until the late 1800's.

Between 1890 and 1920, however, Americans built a new kind of high school education—one consistent with the American way of life and the American pragmatic philosophy. The Kingsley report of 1918, known as the *Cardinal Principles,* repudiated for the high school the 1828 Yale defense of classical tradition. From 1918 to 1954, this new philosophy of education inspired the introduction of courses in swimming, motor vehicle operation, problems of American democracy, and all the great common human interests acceptable to many youths and their parents. These courses are regarded as not quite respectable by those who view education as exclusively concerned with the mind, and by those who have a high regard for the elite selective traditions of Europe.

General Cultural Changes

That changes in educational programs and processes will occur in the last third of the twentieth century is certain. Only the nature of change, not the fact of change, changes, Heraclitus proclaimed almost three millennia ago. Schools exist in a culture and are molded by that culture. It is clear that what happens outside the educational enterprise will be reflected by changes in the schools and colleges.

The first half of the twentieth century has seen a continuing change in population. There are more people—more older people, more younger people, and fewer working people. More Americans are living in cities. New vocations appear almost daily. The introduction of computers and automation requires new labor skills not yet provided for in curriculums of schools and colleges. The rise of nationalism in Africa and Asia, the changed status of women, the awesome power of the atom, and a thousand other developments harass politicians, theologians, economists, and educators.

The issues are basically survival, sovereignty, and sanity. A shrunken planet, the hardware of overkill, and the concept of nation-states and nationalism are the foci of the problems required to be solved or resolved. We must educate the young for the world of twenty years hence; this is the awesome responsibility of today's educators. He who would tinker with that fact of social evolution as a hobby in his spare time is either a knave or a fool. The most important men in America and the world are the educationists, for as Bismarck concluded after the Franco-Prussian War: "He who directs our schools controls our nation's future." Now we would say "the future of the human species." What part the men who devote their professional lives to the study and management of the educational enterprises will have in decision-making, remains to be seen. Education is very much the tool and the weapon of men off campus.

A systematic and complete catalogue of the facts of life of concern to those who build educational systems is beyond the scope of this treatise. These forces are both obvious and subtle. Some are on the surface. Others are deeply buried in the way mankind feels about himself in an ever-expanding universe. The list below will give some notion of the complexity of our world:

1. Atomic power;
2. Mechanization, automation, changed patterns of work;
3. Unequal distribution of resources, gaps in stages of development;
4. Increased leisure time;
5. Divided world, nationalism, blocs, competing philosophies;
6. Dominance of the nation-state, the continuing competition among the big social agencies;
7. "Shrinking" world, the speed of travel and communication;
8. Reckless procreation, differential in birth rates between developed and undeveloped countries and the advantaged and disadvantaged;
9. Urbanization, suburbs, "string" towns;
10. Demotion of man, the individual, the human condition, existential anxiety, addiction to distractions.

Of all these and other social movements, of special importance for those interested in the extracurricular life of students is the increase in leisure time. Modern Americans have time on their hands and it often weighs on their minds.

Among all the many discernible features of the world now, nothing is more clear than this fact that the work-leisure ratio is changing.[1] Americans will play more and work less. (*Work* is used here in the sense of doing what has to be done, not what is chosen to be done.) It was noted earlier that we need fewer farmers, and farmers now do not work from sunup to sundown. The forty-hour five-day work-week is standard—except for executives. Late entry into productive employment, early retirement, and longer paid vacations all contribute to the increase of personally disposable time and the reduction of managed time. The work-time needed to earn a pair of shoes or a pound of meat is very much longer in depressed areas of the globe.

What Americans will do with their free time besides paint their houses inside and out with drip-proof paint will depend on the ways in which the young are educated by schools, magazines, and television. The money spent on cars, boats, and golfclubs exceeds even the expenditures for tobacco and alcohol. Between 1957 and 1960, the gross national product increased 14 per cent. During the same period, expenditures for foreign travel increased 34 per cent; for books and maps, 28 per cent; for theater and opera, 26 per cent; and for community amusements (such as bowling), 30 per cent.

In 1910, most fifteen-year-old children held jobs; in 1930, about 90 per cent of them were in school. Education for the worthy use of leisure time may become more important than education for production. It may be so now. That many student activities are recreation is a fact of institutional life—and a disturbing one to some amateur reformers. It is difficult to reconcile the facts of the new work-leisure balance and the drive to push students through high school and college faster by advanced placement, tri-semester plans, all-year schooling, and the other speedup innovations.

Classical Greece boasted a civilization that set standards no later group has come near attaining. It was built by free men, but the freedom was enjoyed and used at the expense of other men who

---

[1] For a chosen few such as the artist, the man building a business, or the mother, the work-leisure dualism does not exist.

were not free. If schools and colleges can develop interests in the arts, sciences, philosophies, games, and politics, free from money motives and credit-diploma pressures, a new Golden Age is possible for all men.

A too-often-forgotten characteristic of arts, sciences, and games is that they are enjoyed and used, at their best, independently of conflicting philosophies and politics. The Sistine Chapel, the Uffizi Gallery, the Louvre, the Decathlon, the search for causes and cures of cancer, and the great literature of the world are enjoyed without reference to nationality, color, or religion.

The Olympics—a Greek idea—international cultural exchange programs, the vogue of primitive art, and other developments are hopeful signs that what is called the extracurriculum can come to be enjoyed by the many and serve to unite men at home and across frontiers. These and other activities are, for most students, beyond the work necessary to earn diplomas and, for the general population, not a part of the work required to earn a livelihood.

General Educational Developments

After World War II, patriotic Americans took a hard look at education and decided that changes were needed. Automation, population shifts, the new status of women, and a host of other changes had ushered in a new era of transition. The reappraisal, agonized or otherwise, was nothing more nor less than consideration of the question: How will or should society take care of the development and the adjustment needs of the young in the kind of world we will have or want to have? The young must not be adjusted to the world now; they must be made adjustable to the world that will be created and recreated and again made over; for the new is, in our world, newer—and tomorrow it will be new again.

Changes in educational practice have occurred, but always there were those who resisted change. The school is one of our most conservative institutions—and for very good reasons. Schools care for children, the most prized possession of society.

A spoof at critics and reformers of education appeared, incidentally, in a book carrying "some political and economic arguments to their logical conclusion":

But the most rib-tickling *reductio ad absurdum* is the CAI—
"Crusade for Athletic Individualism." The menace of collectivism
as advocated by the Communists threatens our American way of
life, our rugged individualism. None of the sinister Red plots is
more dangerous than the teaching of socialistic team play in sports
to red-blooded American youth. This obviously makes baseball,
football, and basketball dangerous and un-American. Hence, the
CAI attacks all sports "where the individual submerges himself
in the socialistic environment of the team and accepts authoritarian
direction from a captain or some other control apparatus," but
strongly endorses sports like swimming, diving, boxing, and wres-
tling, which "nurture individualism and the spirit of individual enterprise."[2]

It is ridiculous to think that the universal ability to read, speak,
and understand a foreign language or to perform an organic chemi-
cal analysis is the answer to the problems of our species. The problems of mankind are not linguistic, mathematical, or scientific.
When we have enough power to destroy every human twenty times
over, our problem is not nuclear physics. It is something else. The
push for the study of a foreign language by every elementary school
pupil of the land came at a time when the length of time to earn
a Ph.D. and the value of bilingual competency for the degree were
being questioned.

A development, perhaps of epoch-making proportions, of the
1950's and 1960's was the frank alignment of the federal government on the side of physical science and mathematics, and the official acceptance of defense and manpower needs as a concern of
higher education. The Higher Education Facilities Act of 1963
authorized the expenditure of $1.95 billion over the first three
years of a five-year program. Such items as classroom facilities in
the natural or physical sciences, engineering, mathematics, and
foreign language, public junior colleges, and technical institutions
were provided for. Earlier aid under the National Defense Education Act had the same focus. The arts of the arts and sciences
yielded, but not without some protest.

In the American tradition, the schools are run by the people and
serve the values that the people hold most precious. The people

---

[2] Mark Epernay, *The McLandress Dimension* (Boston: Houghton-Mifflin Company, 1963). The book carries come current political and economic arguments
to their insane conclusions. Quoted by William Winter in *The Saturday Review*,
January 18, 1964.

in the 1960's were re-evaluating the education of the young. Between 1960 and some unknown future time, new patterns and new policies will be forged. What these will be and what will happen to the third curriculum nobody can predict. If the past is to any degree a reliable guide, changes will be made in all five large phases of the educational enterprise. Conant[3] proposed, for example, that a foreign language be required of all students in high school who were gifted with an intelligence quotient of 120 or more. Many credit subjects in the elective curriculum, such as driver education, were said to have no place in an educational institution. Even some extracurricular activities, such as music and dramatics, were attacked as being unsuitable educational concerns. Some student services in the fourth curriculum, even medical examinations, were judged to be the responsibility of the home, not of an educational institution. The principle of two credit curriculums, a required and an elective, was not attacked (except indirectly by the recommendation that foreign language, mathematics, and science be moved from the elective to the mandated category for "superior" students).

The hard look at educational programs and processes was not confined to the United States. From England to Indonesia the search for the new world was given high priority. A flattering feature of the worldwide concern with institutional education was the number of individuals and commissions visiting the United States to see what kind of educational programs had helped us to our present levels of abundance and power.

The very concept of education is feeling the stress and strain of the times. It is being redefined. *The educated man, a good education,* and *well-educated* are concepts that have changed through the centuries. The prevailing image of *the educated man* obviously shifts with the dominant values of the age. Those who believe the supreme values lie in military and industrial power had their way in the National Defense Act of 1958, which ignored the humane disciplines. By 1964, there were signs of a counterrevolution.

These facts document the conclusion that determinative educational policy is made by those who manage the nation-state, not by school teachers or professors of education.

A second large feature of the reappraisal of education and a

---

[3] James B. Conant, *The American High School Today* (New York: McGraw-Hill Book Company, Inc., 1959).

phase of the muddy morass of conflicting values was the role of educational institutions. Should schools and colleges be single-purpose or multipurpose institutions? The push for excellence was assumed to refer to intellectual excellence. Productive brain power, mostly in science and technology, was said or implied to be the only purpose of education. Even the Educational Policies Commission used the words *purpose* (in the singular) and *central* in its 1961 dictum.[4] The commission did, of course, point out that *central* did not mean *exclusive*.

To those who believed intellectual goals to be the essence of schooling, the school—though supported by society—was not to be social. A fairly large group held that some ideas were changeless and universal, but that all ideas were best dealt with through words and books and lectures. Hutchins taught that the controlling aim of education was cultivation of the intellect and that this aim was the only true function of education in all ages, all places, and all times.

The National Education Association[5] raised another question:

What are the distinctive responsibilities of the school in contrast to those that properly belong to the family, the church, industry, and various youth-serving agencies?

What responsibilities should the school share with other institutions and agencies?

What, then, should be included in the school program? What should be excluded from it?

Recommendation 10. Priorities for the school are the teaching of skills in reading, composition, listening, speaking (both native and foreign languages), and computation . . . ways of creative and disciplined thinking, including methods of inquiry and application of knowledge, . . . competence in self-instruction and independent learning, . . . fundamental understanding of the humanities and the arts, the social sciences and natural sciences, and mathematics, . . . appreciation of and discriminating taste in literature, music, and the visual arts, . . . instruction in health education and physical education.

Responsibilities best met by joint efforts of the school and other social

---

[4] Educational Policies Commission, *The Central Purpose of Education* (Washington, D.C.: National Education Association, 1961). The National Education Association authorities did see fit to use the reverse page to say, "Publication in this form does not constitute formal approval by the sponsoring associations."

[5] *Schools for the Sixties: IV. Establishing Priorities for the School.* A summary report of the Project on Instruction (Washington, D.C.: National Education Association, 1963).

agencies include: development of values and ideals, . . . social and civic competence, . . . vocational preparation.

The decision to include or exclude particular school subjects or outside-of-class activities should be based on: (a) the priorities assigned to the school and to other agencies; (b) data about learners and society, and developments in the academic disciplines; (c) the human and material resources available in the school and community.

The Association went on to say, in italics:

To determine specifically just what the school's distinctive responsibilities are, each school must find answers to the following questions:
What knowledge, values, and skills do children and youth in our culture need to learn?
Which of these goals can best be achieved by the school?
What knowledge, skills, and values can best be taught by the home, the church, and other social institutions?
Which learnings require the joint efforts of the school and other agencies?

If schools and colleges were to concentrate on, if not be exclusively concerned with, that part of the body which lies above the ears, then good sense would make it necessary to find some other agencies to care for the patriotic, citizenship, recreational, athletic, moral, health, guidance, and emotional needs of the young. That schools and colleges have assumed or been assigned responsibilities beyond the intellectual has long bothered educationists. With too little money and too few troops, these institutions have—for at least five decades—tried to care for the developmental needs of children on a broad spectrum.

School budgets, when reviewed by the district voters or the city council, were found to be overburdened with taxes for transportation, medical care, psychological and psychiatric attention, cafeteria maintenance, guidance services, band uniforms, theater equipment, student unions, uniform cleaning, and a host of other items far removed from the cultivation of rational powers.

The vacuum which would be created by the absurd proposal that nonintellectual matters be made the concern of the home, the parents, and the church cannot be filled except by an agency as large as and more expensive than the public school.

The pragmatic, relativistic pluralism of American democratic and educational thinking had logically turned American hopes to the school—the public school which accepted all the children of all the people and did its best for all the needs that parents in a complex and highly specialized world could not cope with. That this concept of education will be reversed is not probable.

A catalogue of all the other proposals, innovations, new organizations, and new procedures that crowded the columns of the news media and the agendas of educators' conferences during the 1950's and 1960's will give some notion of the extent of the confusion accompanying the search for a better approach. The very number of experimental ventures could lead to the conclusion that this was a panic reaction. It might be that the notice these ventures received in the press was far in excess to their effect on the daily life of the schools. The experimental philosophy and the spirit of reasoned adaption to new demands were also diluted by a bandwagon psychology. It is clear that foreign language instruction in the elementary grades was instituted in many systems only to keep "in the swim."

The following list is incomplete, for many press notices no doubt were missed. Also since new notices appear almost daily, any listing is bound to be out of date.

Evaluation is impossible; nor is it possible to predict which innovation will survive.

Note especially that student activities are not affected except incidentally. In fact, such ideas as independent study programs give students more control over their time.

NEW IDEAS FOR IMPROVEMENT AND ECONOMY IN EDUCATION

Academic time speed up
All-year sessions
Tri-semester plans
Quarter plans
Advance placement
Courses constructed by teams as Physical Science Study Committee
Summer programs
Equivalency examinations
New mathematics programs
New science programs
Examination system (replacing attendance credit)
English examination (instead of class attendance)
Seminars (as for Harvard freshmen)
Learner's credit card
Tutor texts
Team teaching
Paperback books
Teaching machines
Proficiency (equivalency) examinations
Flexible scheduling
Modular scheduling
Independent study

Honors programs
Programmed instruction
Scrambled textbooks
Visiting scholars
Telephone lectures
Foreign language laboratories
Ungraded classes
Ungraded high school
Closed-circuit television
Sunrise television courses

Educational television
Use of radio
Taped drill
Taped lectures by ranking scholars
Reading machines
Teaching machines
Variable class sizes
Voluntary class attendance
Double degrees
School-within-a-school

Student Activities

In this welter of change in the way people live and work, student activities went on with very little new attention. Football games, dances, publications, senior plays, commencement, and all the other activities were enjoyed much as they had been before the reappraisal began. There were continuing concerns with the social life of the young, fraternities, and the place of competitive spectator sports, but student life or "the collegiate way" enjoyed almost complete immunity from new attacks and reform prescriptions. (It should be noted that no entry in the long list of innovations directly affects the student activity program.)

Prediction is precarious at best, but with the change in the rate of change, prediction is sorely needed. A strategically placed observer with some knowledge of the most general features of the prevailing culture and the broad stirrings in the educational enterprise can make some intelligent guesses as to what may happen in the several divisions of the educational institutions.

Prediction does give some light to current controversies, but it cannot control the future. A change in top-level decision-makers[6] can result in widely influential changes in policy. A new President of the United States could, with the help of the military and Congress, build a system of federal schools to siphon off the bothersome 30 to 40 per cent of the high school population. It is clear that American education is culture-bound. Predictions about education therefore imply predictions in the great society of which schools and colleges are only a part.

It is possible to identify some developments which may continue

---

[6] See the changes in North Carolina instituted by Governor Terry Sanford after 1961.

into the not-too-distant future. It should be noted that all items in the list are generally positive to those who believe student activities are an important part of American education. Given the changing work-leisure ratios and the elimination of the rigors of frontier life, Americans must turn to play, games, music, drama, and the other "ennobling" activities, much as did the free classical Greeks in their Golden Age.

Perhaps the word *can* should be used rather than *must*, for the distractions of gambling, alcohol, sex, and shoddy entertainment are always available to persons with time on their hands. Gambling is readily available in many places other than Nevada. New York State legalized bingo and has debated the merits of off-track betting. And it has been seriously proposed that supermarkets be allowed to sell alcoholic beverages.

As clear as anything in the future is the prospect of the continued development of student activities. They will not disappear. In fact, they will increase in variety and in importance. More and more student unions are being built. The many junior and community colleges which were founded in the 1950's and 1960's all made provisions for athletics, sports, and dramatics. Offices for student governments and publications are common facilities.

The same trend is beginning to appear in France, which had been most resistant to the American-British example. The Lycée Pilot at Marseilles had a few arts and crafts clubs and even volleyball courts. (To Americans familiar with French education the sight of boys and girls playing and studying together was a touch of home.)

It is doubtful whether specialized schools for the unsuccessful, the very capable and productive, and those with special interests will be developed. Most schools and colleges in America are small. Only the very largest systems can duplicate the New York City system.

There will be a continuing upgrading of the quality of high school work in dramatics, speech, and music, as well as in athletics. The colleges will lose their traditional dominance in football and basketball to the professional teams. The high schools may provide the outstanding athletic spectacles for public entertainment. There was a time when parents went to school entertainments out of love and duty. In more and more cases, the music and dramatic productions are approaching professional quality.

It was suggested earlier that the advisor to the student council needs special training. The trend toward specialization has been slow in public education, but the pace could very well quicken. Colleges are giving many courses to prepare future teachers in specialized activities.

Provision for youth recreation has grown with almost no over-all communitywide planning. Churches, Y's, boys' clubs and other noncommercial agencies compete with commercial sports palaces. The schools dominate the field, but such activities as bowling, skiing, motion pictures, and "charm" schools are left to commercial agencies. The government generally makes provision for camping, swimming, hunting, and fishing activities. No hope can be entertained that coordinated, unified, citywide programs will be developed. There will be duplication of facilities and competition for patronage. The Public Schools of Kansas have united in encouraging and controlling student activities on a wide front through their Kansas State High School Activities Association. The officers of the association work closely with the State Education Department in Topeka.

Such voluntary associations may become the pattern in the future. Whether centralization in larger and larger units is desirable is a debatable issue. The American concept of equality, combined with the dominance of the state and federal governments in taxing power over the local communities will inevitably cause local authorities to look to the larger governmental units for funds.

That there will be more student travel as the years go by is fairly certain. Travel for pleasure and learning is made increasingly easy and inexpensive. Washington, New York, Montreal, Mexico City, and the beaches of Florida are crowded with high school and college students during spring vacations. International travel agencies are thriving.

Painting, sculpture, and the other arts will most certainly attract the attention of more students and their school authorities. Creative expression in dramatics, dance, and writing may serve as an antidote for a world too difficult to understand. In the past the school has often been hostile to the aspiring creator. The young poet was made to repeat freshman mathematics four times. That may change —at least there are faint signs that *gifted* is being more broadly and sensibly interpreted.

Students' lives center about the school. It is a rare weekend that the school is not crowded with students and their suburban parents. After-school activities are common. Buses run all day long and on Friday and Saturday evenings. Many communities have Sunday athletic contests and Sunday family swimming in the pools. This trend will continue.

In Harvard's policy of using "a touch of greatness" or some combination of "effectiveness, energy, judgment, integrity, generosity of spirit" as a supplement to college board tests for admission may be seen a trend to a more systematic appraisal of personal abilities that are better developed and evaluated in student activities than in strictly academic endeavors. The ability to think, to work with others, to assume leadership, to hold fast to the fundamental moral and democratic values in the face of pressure, to be an individual are requirements for success in student activities. Techniques for evaluation and for development are not now available, but attention will be given in the future to this long-neglected aspect of personality.

The trends suggested above, it will be noted, are generally positive. They see the future as growing better and better. No perfectionism should be assumed, for there are grave problems ahead and humanity's best thinking always outreaches its grasp. America was built on faith in man and in his ability to make his future all that it could and ought to be. The gradual cosmic demotion of man and his planet—however much it may have induced abandonment of hope in adults—has failed to convince the young that there was not fun to be had in living. Youth, it appears, has a wisdom and a will all its own. Adults must learn to trust the young, to teach them concern for the welfare of all men on a personal and planetary scale, and to guide their actions in the conviction that the future will indeed be bright.

Bibliography

Allen, Charles Forrest, *Outlines of Extra-Curricular Activities*. Little Rock, Ark.: High School Print Shop, May, 1924.

Allen, Henry A., *Extra-Curricular Activities*. Boston: D. C. Heath & Company, 1926.

Berry, C. A., *Activities and Citizenship*. 1951 Yearbook, National Council for the Social Studies, 1951.

Borgeson, Frithiof Carl, *Elementary School Life Activities*. New York: A. S. Barnes & Co., 1931.

Cox, Phillip Westcott Lawrence, *Creative School Control*. Philadelphia: J. B. Lippincott Company, 1927.

Deam, Thomas M. and Olive M. Bear, *Socializing the Pupil Through Extra-Curricular Activities*. Chicago: Benjamin H. Sanborn & Co., 1928.

Eby, Frederick, *The Development of Modern Education*, rev. ed. Englewood Cliffs, N.J.: Prentice-Hall, Inc., 1952.

Fedder, Ruth, *Guiding Homeroom and Club Activities*. New York: McGraw-Hill Book Company, 1949.

Foster, Charles R., *Extra-Curricular Activities in the High School*. Richmond, Va.: Johnson Publishing Co., 1925.

Frederick, Robert W., *The Third Curriculum*. New York: Appleton-Century-Crofts, Inc., 1959.

Fretwell, Elbert K., *Extracurricular Activities in Secondary Schools*. Boston: Houghton Mifflin Company, 1931.

Gruber, Frederick C. and Thomas Bayard Beatty, *Secondary School Activities*. New York: McGraw-Hill Book Company, 1954.

Hand, Harold C., *Principal Findings of the 1947–1948 Basic Studies of the Illinois Secondary School Curriculum Program*, Circular Series A, No. 51. Springfield, Ill.: State Education Department, 1949.

Holroyd, George Henry, *The Organization of School Societies and Other School Activities*. London: Sir Isaac Pitman & Sons, Ltd., 1933.

Johnson, Mary Hooker, *The Dean in the High School*. New York: Professional and Technical Press, 1929.

Johnston, Edgar Grant and Roland C. Faunce, *Student Activities in Secondary Schools*. New York: The Ronald Press Co., 1952.

Jones, Anna May, *Leisure Time Education*, A Handbook of Creative Activities for Teachers and Group Leaders. New York: Harper & Row, Publishers, 1946.

Jordon, R. H., *Extra-Classroom Activities*. New York: The Macmillan Company, 1927.

Kilzer, L. R., H. H. Stephenson, and H. O. Nordberg, *Allied Activities in the Secondary School*. New York: Harper & Row, Publishers, 1956.

MacDonald, Margaret Ann, *The Class Organization and Activities*. New York: A. S. Barnes & Co., 1931.

McKown, Harry Charles, *Extra-Curricular Activities,* 3rd ed. New York: The Macmillan Company, 1952.

————, *Activities in the Elementary School.* New York: McGraw-Hill Book Comanpy, 1938.

————, *School Clubs.* New York: The Macmillan Company, 1929.

Meyer, Harold Diedrich, *The School Club Program.* New York: A. S. Barnes, & Co., 1931.

————, *A Handbook of Extra-Curricular Activities in the High School.* New York: A. S. Barnes & Co., 1926.

Millard, C. V., *The Organization and Administration of Extra-Curricular Activities.* New York: A. S. Barnes & Co., 1930.

Miller, Franklin A., James H. Moyer, and Robert B. Patrick, *Planning Student Activities.* Englewood Cliffs, N.J.: Prentice-Hall, Inc., 1956.

Mock, Albert, *The Extracurricular Manual.* Indianapolis, Ind.: Published by the author, 1950.

National Association of Secondary School Principals, *Vitalizing Student Activities in the Secondary School,* Vol. 36, No. 184 (February 1952).

————, *Student Activities in the Secondary School,* Vol. 28, No. 119 (January 1944).

National Society for the Study of Education, *The Activity Movement.* 33rd Yearbook, Part II, Bloomington, Ill.: Public School Publishing Co., 1934.

————, *Extra-Curricular Activities.* 25th Yearbook, Part II, Bloomington, Ill.: Public School Publishing Co., 1926.

Otto, Henry John and Shirley A. Hamrin, *Co-Curricular Activities in Elementary Schools.* New York: Appleton-Century-Crofts, Inc., 1937.

Pierce, Anna Eloise, *Deans and Advisors of Women and Girls.* New York: Professional and Technical Press, 1928.

Pound, Olivia, *Extra-Curricular Activities of High School Girls.* New York: A. S. Barnes & Co., 1931.

Reavis, W. C. and G. R. Van Dyke, "Non-Athletic Extra-Curriculum Activities," *National Survey of Secondary Education,* Bulletin No. 17, 1932, Monograph No. 26, Washington, D.C.: USGPO, 1933.

Remmers, H. H. (ed.), *Studies in Extracurricular Activities.* Lafayette, Ind.: Purdue University Press, 1950.

Robert, A. C. and E. M. Draper, *Extraclass and Intramural Activities in High Schools.* Boston: D. C. Heath & Company, 1928.

Roemer, Joseph, C. F. Allen, and Dorothy A. Yarnell, *Basic Student Activities: Organization and Administration of Homerooms, Clubs, and Assemblies.* New York: Silver Burdett Company, 1935.

Roemer, Joseph, and Charles Forrest Allen, *Readings in Extra-Curricular Junior and Senior High Schools.* Boston: D. C. Heath & Company, 1926.

Roemer, Joseph, and Charles Forrest Allen, *Readings in Extra-Curricular Activities.* Richmond, Va.: Johnson Publishing Co., 1929.

Index

Index